Here are the words I would use to describe my dear friend Dorothy Newton: courageous, strong, beautiful, and Christ-honoring. She bravely tells her story of abuse to encourage others that even in the midst of heartbreak and pain, God is faithful. You can survive brokenness, and the key is knowing the One who was broken and bruised for all mankind—Jesus.

Joni Lamb, vice president and cofounder of Daystar Television Network

We applaud Dorothy for bearing her soul in this book. It is a moving and emotional account of a difficult journey and her unyielding devotion to God and family.

Kelvin and Lynn Martin, former wide receiver for the Dallas Cowboys

We've been friends with Dorothy Newton for years and have long admired her strength and courage. She's a devoted mother who after her divorce brought that family together and held them so tightly that nothing could have ever torn them apart. It was incredibly touching and inspiring to watch. She is also one of the most spiritual people we've ever met, something she leaned on for strength during the trials of her marriage. She has a lifetime of wisdom to impart, and the simple, straightforward way she does so here makes every page an inspiration. It's a book filled with love, perseverance, and proof that in America, second acts aren't only for men; women have some pretty remarkable ones as well.

Emmitt Smith, NFL Hall of Famer
Pat Smith, founder/CEO of Treasure You

It is a privilege to call Dorothy Newton friend. Her life is an inspiring example of a courageous woman of God who values faith, family, and friends as our ultimate early treasures. She shares her past and present experiences with others in the hope that they too can celebrate life in abundance now and forever.

Pat and Cheri Summerall, now-deceased legendary television sportscaster

My friend Dorothy Newton will become your friend as she graciously takes you into her world—into the celebrity lifestyle and the shadowy recesses where abuse dominated and destroyed her dream world. She shares mistakes and victories. She contrasts the voice of abuse, which shouts fear and shame, with the sweet song of freedom and healing. In *Silent Cry*, you will be encouraged to not let your pain define you or your future. I have no doubt that getting to know Dorothy Newton will enrich and encourage

*Debbie Mo̶   Women) at
G̶   ̶sed Woman*

Though the book's title reads *Silent Cry*, this is a story about triumph and grace—the triumph of Dorothy, of her sons Tré and King, and ultimately of Nate Newton as well. Both the good and the bad we read in this story occur beneath the covering of God's grace, which is the bedrock of Dorothy's strength. In fact, this book is more than a story; it is a witness and full evidence of human capability. Every man should read this biography."

Monte Ford, former senior vice president at American Airlines
Ingrid Ford, owner of Peace of Life Massage

Powerful. Straightforward. Honest. Brave. These are words I use to describe Dorothy Newton. When I first met her, I knew immediately there was a spiritual strength about her that was uncommon. However, it wasn't until she dared to share the story of *Silent Cry* with me that I fully understood how her ability to overcome personal pain had been shaped by her passion for Jesus. Dorothy chose in the midst of isolation and relational deprivation to turn her tears into floods of victory. She shares the truth of her personal story in a way that reveals hope for anyone dealing with difficult circumstances, unhealthy relationships, or even devastating loss. It is rare to find such honesty and hope in the same place. If you've ever wondered how you are going to make it, this book is for you.

Jan Greenwood, pastor, Pink (Gateway Women) at
Gateway Church and author of *Women at War*

Beauty, honesty, and guts describe this overcomer named Dorothy Newton. Because of Dorothy's courage to tell her story, all of us will better understand the horrible reality of domestic violence in our own backyard. We'll discover that all of us are responsible to learn about it, fight it, and give others a way out when they need it. Most of all, this true story will help victims know without a doubt that with God, they can escape domestic abuse and rise above it.

Lisa Rose, founder and board president of The Gatehouse,
a ministry for women and children in crisis

Truth brings liberty to the captive, gives beauty for ashes, great joy in place of grieving, and high praise to God instead of despair. Dorothy is a living testimony of this. She shares this story courageously so that the reader can experience God in their own set of circumstances. She found her tears and her freedom. Come, dear reader, and find yours too.

Rebecca Wilson, LCSW, LMFT, pastor, Marriage and
Family Ministries at Gateway Church

Silent Cry

Silent Cry

THE TRUE STORY OF ABUSE AND BETRAYAL OF AN NFL WIFE

DOROTHY J. NEWTON

ZONDERVAN

Silent Cry
Copyright © 2015 by Dorothy J. Newton

Silent Cry is written in collaboration with Wendy K. Walters.

This title is also available as a Zondervan ebook. Visit www.zondervan.com/ebooks.

Requests for information should be addressed to:
Zondervan, 3900 *Sparks Dr. SE, Grand Rapids, Michigan 49546*

ISBN 978-0-310-34484-1

Cover design: Curt Diepenhorst
Cover photography: Dan Davis
Interior design: Kait Lamphere

First Printing July 2015 / Printed in the United States of America

To all who have suffered betrayal and abuse.
To all who need deliverance and freedom.
To all who hope ...

I have been crucified with Christ;
it is no longer I who live,
but Christ lives in me;
and the life which I now live in the flesh
I live by faith in the Son of God,
who loved me
and gave Himself for me.

Galatians 2:20 NKJV

Contents

Part 4: A Troubled Marriage

Part 5: Moving On

Foreword

You can tell a lot about someone by looking into his or her eyes. Some eyes sparkle with life, some seem far away and distracted, while others are deep pools of sadness. Eyes can tell a story that the heart would find difficult to put into words.

I remember the first time I looked into Dorothy's eyes. She was a guest at a Christmas production I was hosting, and I was introduced to her at the meet and greet at the end of the evening. Her elegant beauty and lovely smile were what struck me initially—but it was the depth of what I saw in her eyes that stayed with me. As I drove home that night, I prayed for her. I knew nothing of her story, but I saw something I recognized. I saw the familiar weight of one who has walked a long, hard road and gathered the rare fruit of profound empathy that only such a path can produce. Grace rested in her eyes.

When this manuscript came across my desk, I was excited to read her story. It's a hard story to read. Dorothy's life has been marked by pain and abuse since she was a child. If that sounds warning bells deep inside you, don't pull back; there is so much more here that you need to know.

She is honest and transparent about a time when it was almost impossible for a woman to be heard and taken seriously, particularly if she was married to a powerful man. We live in a culture that worships and elevates our sports stars but doesn't love them enough to help them when they are clearly in trouble. When we attempt to contain and manage the rage that rests inside some of our heroes, we do them a disservice, and we abandon those who need us most — their wives and children. I pray that Dorothy's courage in telling her story will be a catalyst for change.

More than anything, this is a story of redemption and hope. No matter how deep the pit you find yourself in might be, the love of God is deeper still. No matter how many poor choices you might have made, His mercies are new every morning.

If you are a woman living in a desperate situation, you will find help in these pages. You are not alone. If you know of someone who is being abused, this book will give you very practical steps to know how to help. If you are the abuser, there is hope and healing for you as well. It's never too late to throw yourself on the grace and mercy of God and begin the slow but sure process of learning to live differently.

I highly recommend this book. It's heartbreaking to think that Dorothy had to endure so much for so long, and yet what shines through her story is a spiritual truth of which I am convinced: It's amazing what God can do with a broken life if you give Him all the pieces.

Sheila Walsh

Preface

In an online article published December 4, 2012, at Slate.com, journalist Justin Peters candidly revealed some amazing statistics about the NFL teams active in the 2012 season. Twenty-one of the thirty-two football teams had at least one player with a domestic violence or sexual assault charge on his record. Further sources at the time cited evidence that professional athletes, as a whole, were not being punished as harshly as the general public — by almost half. News reports in 2014 showed that abuse by members of the NFL was getting more coverage, and courts seemed to be taking the issue more seriously. For that, I am grateful.

My story began before anything on the subject popped up on Google. I lived in a secret world where abuse by my former husband, a professional football player, left me feeling helpless and isolated. I survived without benefit from any source of relief and, in many instances, without protection. Allow me to say that my story is not meant to attack anyone's character, but rather to record one woman's dependencies on a sovereign God who sees, knows, and understands the depths of despair. It is also the story of a God who desires to deliver and walk alongside each of us to a place of wholeness and freedom.

I've tried to be as honest as is humanly possible about Nate, my circumstances, and myself. I sincerely believe the truth does indeed set us free. I've worked to be transparent about the nature of abuse patterns and the reality that their ugly legacies pass from one generation to the next. I got the false impression in my childhood that abuse and violence are to be considered normal in a family atmosphere. And I've tried to understand how witnessing such events as a young girl opened the door for my relationship with Nate.

The general purpose of gathering years of material to write *Silent Cry* was twofold. First, I am endeavoring to encourage those who stand in the shadow of prominent figures in our American culture to take the risk of reaching out for help. Second, I want to bring hope, healing, and wholeness to those who are suffering in silence. I believe there is a way out, and God will help you find it. He can hear your silent cry.

Dorothy J. Newton

Acknowledgments

To my mother, Ethel (Keeby) —

You are a strong woman of God and an evangelist, the oldest of thirteen children, a mother, a friend, and a sister. You worked hard your entire life and never gave up, even with limitations in education. You taught me perseverance even in the midst of the storm. I am proud that you finally received your high school diploma in 2008.

To my siblings, Gary, Muriel, Helaine, John, and Leslie —

I ask for your understanding and forgiveness. By choosing to privately absorb all the hurt and pain, I denied you the opportunity to lift me up and feel the satisfaction of being there for me as you often were gracious enough to let me be there for you. After all, we are blessed to be a blessing. You were only allowed to see the part of me I wanted you to see. I thought I was protecting you by not burdening you with problems. I was so wrong. In retrospect, your collective strengths surely would have changed my course and perhaps yours too — bringing us even closer than we already are. Please know how much I love each of you. I give you my word that I promise to depend on you for all the times that lie ahead—both good and bad. It's never too late to lead an authentic and full life.

To my brother, Mike—

Though we didn't grow up together, we spent time talking on the phone in college. I was privileged to attend a couple of your pro games and honored to be there when you married your beautiful wife, Deidre. When Dad was diagnosed with cancer, you took excellent care of him in your home, and I enjoyed visiting with you when I came to see him. This was when I really got to know you, and it felt as if I had known you my whole life. You are an amazing and intelligent man who always prioritized God first, then family, and then being a professional athlete. Pro football was always what you did, not who you were—and I admire this. I do not see you as a stepbrother; you are my brother, and I love you.

In memory of—

My stepfather: Lester Hymes
February 28, 1943–May 10, 1983

My stepsister: Mary Hymes
August 19, 1960–July 30, 1983

My father: Horris Lee Johnson
June 25, 1940–April 10, 2010

Acknowledgments

With gratitude to all who contributed in important ways to the journey that culminated in Silent Cry —

I am forever grateful to Marcus and Joni Lamb at Daystar Television. Participating in "Joni Table Talk" has contributed to my spiritual growth and has helped me greatly to keep life in perspective. Joni, you are a treasure as a friend!

Life doesn't happen without prayer, and I owe deep and abiding gratitude to my prayer partner and friend Freda Dents.

I would be remiss if I failed to offer heartfelt thanks to Wendy K. Walters, who so graciously came alongside me and helped me put my words on paper and bring my story to life. For her colabor in love, I will always be grateful.

Additional thanks goes to my fellow author Melanie Stiles for believing in my cause, upholding me in prayer, and supporting my endeavors, and to Brenda Claborn, a tireless advocate who believed from the beginning that my story needed to be told and who pointed me to John Sloan at Zondervan to make this publication possible.

An abundance of thanks to my entire Zondervan team. Although they are numerous, I'd like to single out Dirk Buursma, John Sloan, Alicia Kasen, and Curt Diepenhorst. You've done an excellent and professional job, and I really appreciate it!

Finally and foremost, I thank God for opening this window of opportunity.

PART 1

Childhood

CHAPTER 1

The Storm

Living is strife and torment,
disappointment and love and sacrifice,
golden sunsets and black storms.

Laurence Olivier

September 1965. Tornado sirens wail their warning as ominous dark clouds gather overhead. Hurricane Betsy is fast approaching, promising damage and destruction to everything in her path.

I look around our small trailer. This is home to my mom, stepfather, me, and my brothers and sisters. Every room is a bedroom, but only three tiny rooms hold the official title. The place is crowded, and we take up every square inch of space. I sense my mother's anxiety growing, but my four-year-old mind can't fully comprehend why. She is packing at a feverish pace, shoving belongings into a few small suitcases. I glance at the overhead compartments in the hallway. They hold precious new pencils, notebooks, and art supplies we need for the new school year. Why isn't Mother packing these? What about my pillow? Surely we can't leave without my Easy-Bake Oven! Where are we going anyway? The sirens seem to be getting closer and closer, and I cover my ears to shut them out.

I grab my mother's sleeve as she squeezes a suitcase together and then snaps it shut. I ask her about my Easy-Bake Oven. She pauses mid-frenzy, attempting to focus calm attention in my direction. She strokes my hair and cups her hand beneath my chin, explaining that we can take only what we can carry. Tears well up in her eyes, and she closes them for a brief moment, quickly wiping the tears away before they spill down her cheeks. We don't have a car, so our only means of escape is public transportation.

We board a school bus heading for shelter at a navy base located in Belle Chase, Louisiana. My mother leads the way. My stepfather is a pace behind, his leg in a cast, and four small children under the age of five scramble to keep up with both of them while carrying all that our little arms could hold.

We huddle closely to my mother, who instinctively herds us together for safety. I am afraid. I don't understand the word *uncertainty*, but I feel the weight of it. The storm takes the shape of a menacing villain—and it is out to get us. *Will it follow us? When can we go home? Will my things still be there for me to play with?*

My mother does her best to be calm, repeatedly telling us that everything will be alright. But her eyes constantly sweep across the parking lot, searching the horizon for something … only she knows what.

When the storm finally passed, our family was safe, but we had no home to return to. All that remained of our possessions was contained in a few suitcases. We were homeless. For a short season, we took up shelter with various relatives. School started up again, but I was no longer excited about it. In fact, I was frightened to leave my mother and cried every day, begging her to let me stay with her. She tried to calm my fears and reassure me by accompanying me to Ms. Stivinson's class. Ms. Stivinson would then place me on her lap, smile sweetly, and tell me in a soft, reassuring voice how nicely I was dressed or how pretty I was. In time, her kindness melted my fears, and my discomfort dissolved into trust.

Eventually, we did have our own place again, but there were still dark clouds on the horizon. Hurricane Betsy wasn't the only storm I had to navigate early in life. Another tempest was brewing, and the damage this one threatened was much more devastating than loss of property. My stepfather drank. And whenever he drank too much, he became violent. Every day, he fought with my mother, hurling physical, verbal, and emotional blows that bruised her body, mind, and soul. I did my best to shut out the abuse by pretending it wasn't happening, but it sickened me. I had no idea how to escape, but I began to dream we all would one day fly away from him and go somewhere where we could live—happy and free.

In spite of the abuse, my mother was a strong woman, and she took very good care of us. By 1970, we were a family with six children, and no matter how unhappy or trapped she felt, she was determined to instill good values and morals into our fragile, young minds.

On Sundays, she dressed us in our best outfits and sent us walking down a country road to Pilgrim Rest Baptist Church. Other children fidgeted during service, drew on church bulletins, and whispered their way through Sunday sermons—but not me. For me, church was a haven. People there were kind, and I loved to go to church. My Sunday school teacher, Ms. Pinkins, allowed me to read Scripture aloud for the class and to record attendance. This made me feel special and important. By the time I was eight, she taught me how to handle tithe envelopes, count money, and keep records in the church book.

And then it happened again. A ferocious storm named Hurricane Camille hit Louisiana, Mississippi, and the Gulf Coast in August 1969, threatening to uproot us once more. However, this time, though our home and Pilgrim Rest Baptist Church were damaged, all was not lost. The evacuation was shorter, and it wasn't long before things were repaired and in some ways better than ever.

I continued to thrive and take on new responsibilities at church. By the age of ten, I was the designated narrator for Christmas and Easter plays. One Sunday, I was asked to give the welcome address for our minister, Reverend Hardy, before he preached his sermon. This led to invitations from other churches to tell Bible stories, read Scripture, and even to lead the choir in singing the classic hymn, "In the Garden." At times, I traveled with my sisters Muriel and Helaine as far as sixty miles to New Orleans or across the river to Pointe à la Hache to be welcomed as guests of other churches.

No matter how difficult things were at home, church filled me with joy. I was safe and happy there. Scripture took on meaning and filtered through my adolescent mind to influence my thoughts and choices. I understood the importance of prayer and supplication and knew I could bring my requests to God daily. Of course, the one thing I asked for most was for my parents to stop arguing and for my stepfather to stop drinking. My relationship with God became the most important thing in my life. His overwhelming love for me would sustain me through all the storms yet to come.

CHAPTER 2

Keeby's Kids

A parent's love is whole no matter
how many times divided.

Robert Brault

My biological father was out of my life by the time I turned three. The only daddy I ever really knew was my stepfather, Lester. When he married my mother, she had three small children. In no time, more little ones came along, and three children became six. Gary was the oldest, then me, followed by Muriel, Helaine, John, and finally Leslie. Ten short years spanned the difference between the oldest and youngest child, so when we lined up in a row, we literally looked like little stair steps.

Each day, my stepfather woke up and faithfully went to his job as a crane operator. He made a decent living, and for a long season, things were pretty good for us financially. Lester was a man of simple tastes, and when he came home, my mother always had something hearty and piping hot waiting for him to eat. I remember fondly the smell of red beans and rice simmering on the stove, our little trailer in spotless order, all the clothes washed and ironed, and my mother having everything just so in time for his arrival home.

My mother's given name was Ethel, but everyone called her Keeby. She worked hard to make sure her family was well mannered and well-thought-of. In the early days, when money was available, she had our clothing made for us. Sometimes she would take us to New Orleans to shop for clothes. Those were good, good times. She was so proud to see her children in nice things. Everybody called us "Keeby's Kids," and we were always dressed in matching outfits. We knew how to behave ourselves, mind our manners, be respectful of our elders, and make a good impression wherever we went. My mother smiled from ear to ear when people commented on how well behaved we were. We loved seeing her smile, and that was reward enough. As the oldest of thirteen children, my mother learned how to cook, clean, and take care of a family at a young age. By third grade, she dropped out of school to stay at home to help take care of her brothers and sisters. She didn't have an opportunity to learn how to read and could barely write her name, but she carried herself with dignity and authority. She was intelligent and always conducted her business as aptly as any professional woman. She commanded great respect everywhere she went. When she took me with her to the store to fill out checks, it never occurred to me that she couldn't do it for herself. I thought she was just teaching me how to do it so I could learn. The same was true when she asked me to read Scripture out loud in the evenings. Oh, how she loved the Bible! I never dreamed she asked me because she couldn't read.

Because my mother was such a gifted and respected communicator, few people knew her secret. It wasn't until I was in high school and asked for her help with an algebra problem one night that I discovered the extent of her limitations. I was forced to swallow the bitter pill of my mother's illiteracy, and I was shocked. In my eyes, she had always been brilliant. However, when I realized how much she had accomplished in spite of this huge obstacle, I respected her even more.

Like all the women in our family, she was strong—she had to be. Others depended on her, and she wouldn't let them down, no matter what. Ours was definitely a matriarchal culture. The women established the moral and religious structure for the family. They set the rules, provided the discipline, and taught the lessons. They were the glue that held everyone together, kept our spirits high in hard times, and created a community that cared deeply for each other and looked after its own. And there were plenty of us to look after.

Eleven of my aunts and uncles lived less than a quarter mile from our home. Even the smallest occasion was a reason to gather, make mountains of food, and spend long afternoons talking and playing with cousins. No one had a large home. In fact, most of us lived in trailers. To this day, I can't quite remember how we managed to get everyone together in one place for a giant Louisiana-style crawfish boil, but we did. It was wonderful! For Christmas, we all gathered at Grandma's house. Everyone brought something to eat, and we got all dressed up in our Sunday best. There was love and laughter and practical jokes and family gossip and drama — it was crazy and crowded and absolutely the most wonderful time you can imagine. I loved spending time with my family, and I felt very special to be part of them. It was the only life I ever knew — a life filled with people who cared about you, shared your joys and your sorrows, picked you up when you were down, and made life worth living. And God was in the center of my immediate family. Our faith in him was solid.

My aunts were especially good to me. Auntie Melvina threw parties and often made treats for me and my friends. Auntie Helen took the best clothes out of her closet for me to wear on special occasions. Over the years, Auntie Dee Dee called to check on me and sent me letters. Auntie Red made my favorite foods as a treat and occasionally gave me just a little something that made me feel special.

For a variety of reasons, I began to experience tension with my younger siblings during this time. Being singled out for special assignments at church and school meant I had privileges they didn't. To make matters worse, I got good grades and was popular at school. Because I was the oldest girl in the family, it was also my job to help the younger ones with homework, make sure everything was taken care of for school, and be the disciplinarian when necessary. My "rank" clearly annoyed my siblings. They called me "Goody Two-Shoes" and "Miss Bossy." When they were really irritated with me, they called me "Pie Face"—or the one I hated most (and they knew it): "Miss Princess La-La."

Without really understanding why, I pulled away from my siblings and looked instead to my aunts for companionship, particularly my auntie Dee Dee. She had gotten married when she was just eighteen and moved away to California. Even though she was far away, she wrote me letters, encouraged me to do well in school, and counseled me about things in my life that troubled me. She was my link to a world bigger than our small Louisiana community, and I was hungry to discover things outside our little circle.

I knew I was destined for greater things. I believed God had a purpose for my life that was bigger than anything I could yet imagine. And yet there was a shadow lurking—a dark shadow that cast its coldness over everything warm and beautiful and good.

CHAPTER 3

Evil Drink

Wine hath drowned more
men than the sea.

Thomas Fuller

My stepfather, Lester, was a wonderful, loving man—until he drank. I often wondered if the alcohol revealed his true nature, or if the drink itself was responsible for his vicious behavior. Though I can't remember a single day he didn't get up and go to work, as I got older, there were fewer and fewer nights he came home right after work. Instead, he went into town and poured himself into a bottle until nothing of his gentle nature remained.

The good times became careful times. The careful times became difficult times, and it wasn't long until we were in really bad shape. Lester continued working every day, but money stopped coming into the household. Liquor led to gambling. The greater the losses at the gambling table, the greater his need for alcohol. He stumbled home late at night, filled to the brim with rage, and took out his frustrations on my mother.

She tried everything to calm him down—fixing him hot food in the middle of the night, figuring out what she had done to displease him, and trying to change herself in hopes of somehow making him better. It wasn't long until evidence of extramarital affairs appeared, and when my mother confronted him, things got even worse. The more his life spun out of control, the more he fought to dominate and control our little world at home. Abuse became an everyday reality, and my mother was locked in the crosshairs of his anger and violence.

When there was no longer enough money even for food, my mother began looking for work. Because she couldn't read,

I went with her to help her fill out job applications. After weeks of searching, she landed a job as a custodian at our school in Buras, Louisiana. It was the only school in town, and everyone from kindergarteners through high school seniors attended there. My mother was so excited to have a job and make her own money. She could work during the same hours we were in school and then be home with us when school let out.

In order to stretch our meager budget, my mother supplemented our meals with scraps she brought home from the school cafeteria. She wasn't stealing, mind you. She brought home only what the children threw away. She prayed over it, cut off any edges that had bite marks, and developed creative ways to turn this castaway cuisine into something we could survive on. When I discovered what she was doing, I was horrified and disgusted. At the time, I didn't see it as resourceful and brave. I didn't understand how committed she was to our survival—no matter what.

My mother scrimped and was frugal, but she also loved to be generous whenever she could. I will never forget the first Christmas after she had a job. We rarely received Christmas presents or birthday gifts, but my mother had carefully saved a portion of each paycheck until she had enough money to buy something special for each of us. My sisters and I received monogram rings, and the boys each got a bicycle. I'll never know how she did it, but she found a way. No matter how tight money was or how tired she was from working or fending off my stepfather, she always found ways to do special things for us and express her love for us.

～～

Living in a small, close-knit community meant everyone knew everyone else's business. When my stepfather came home raging in the middle of the night, my siblings and I sometimes tried to step in and mediate. On many occasions, one or more of us would run outside and plead for help. My older brother Gary wanted desperately to protect Mother, but he was no match for our stepfather.

Our relatives and neighbors would try to answer our cries when the fight was on, and sometimes the police would come, but my stepfather held some inexplicable power over all of them. Whenever he started talking, it was like he cast a magic spell on people. Though the evidence of the abuse was as plain as day, and we had been there to witness it all, he was always able to explain it all away. Because he had a reputation as a hard worker and was loved and respected by everyone, no one wanted to believe he was capable of such violence. His behavior toward my mother so contradicted the "daytime version" of his life that it left our family and neighbors just as confused about him as we were.

Somehow, what happened in our home was considered a private matter between a man and his wife — therefore, it should not be interfered with. It was like some unspoken code. There was a deeply ingrained, dangerous tolerance for domestic violence in our community. The women shook their heads in sympathy and prayed silently — too many of them had also been victims of violence at one time or another.

I coped by throwing myself into my schoolwork, carving out a place for myself in the top tiers of my class. I was involved in everything a student could possibly be involved in, and Buras High School was my haven. My drive to succeed went far beyond the classroom. I learned to channel the frustrations of my home life into the positive energy of competitive athletics, where my focus and natural abilities soon brought me to the front of the pack.

The problem was that participating in athletics cost money, and I needed to pay for everything from tennis shoes and uniforms to registration fees and travel. By this time, we had even less money to live on, and my mother's salary didn't allow for any extras. I felt guilty having to ask her for money to purchase what I needed. Sometimes she had to take out small loans to keep us kids supplied. Because of her good reputation and kindness, people were often willing to lend a helping hand. But as I grew older and was increasingly aware of our plight, I often pretended I didn't need anything so I could somehow lighten her burden.

I had a friend named Deborah who played sports with me. Her mother was a friend to my mother and was aware of our situation. When we had out-of-town games, Deborah often paid for my meal or ordered double portions and pretended she couldn't eat it all so she could share with me. Her generosity melted some of the hardness that had developed around my heart. God used her compassion to reveal his love to me. Over and over again, the warmth of Deborah's kindness melted the cold, hard knot growing within me, allowing me to trust God and know I was in his hands.

Sometimes, no matter how hard she tried, Mother couldn't find the money for the things I needed. When times were really desperate, she'd get a faraway look in her eyes, sigh deeply, and say, "I guess you'll have to ask your daddy." I'm not sure how he found the money or even why he did it, but he always seemed to come up with what I needed so I could continue to play sports and be involved in all my academic and extracurricular activities.

At softball games, I sometimes saw my stepfather standing off by himself in the distance. He never came into the stands. He didn't want to be around people, but he was there watching.

When it was my turn at bat, I would think, *Come on, Dot, hit this one right over his head!* I wanted to make a ball fly right over his head to get his attention!

I played basketball and volleyball too, but he never came to a single game. Those sports were played inside a gym, and I think the idea of coming inside and being around people was just too much for him. I sometimes wondered if he was ashamed of himself. I hoped he was. More than anything, I wanted him to stop drinking. I knew he could be a good man — he just refused to give up alcohol.

There were times when the abuse did stop momentarily. Maybe that meant he had a winning streak at gambling — I never knew for sure. When things were really, really bad, my Uncle Sam could actually put him in his place and cause him to back down, even to express remorse. But this lasted only for a day or two, and then the abuse began all over again. It was like living inside a nightmare I couldn't wake up from. It seemed normal. I expected it. I got used to it. That's just how it was. There wasn't anything to do but accept it.

No matter how we begged him to stop or pleaded for his goodness to return, it never did. The abuse continued and got steadily worse. My mother began to have frequent seizures and constant, severe headaches. Several times his blows landed her in the hospital, and I feared my mother would sooner or later die at his hands.

Finally we realized there was nothing left to do but escape — and the only way to do that was to become self-sufficient. I was in the ninth grade by now, and my brother Gary and I had begun to chip in, working to help support the family. I worked every weekend cleaning houses or picking bushels of beans. I even worked at a shrimp factory, plucking the heads off the tiny creatures and filling buckets with them. How I hated those slimy things! They smelled horrible, and the stench lingered long after I got home and took a bath. It seemed like I could smell them even in my sleep. The outer shells of the shrimp scraped my fingers, and I worked until they were raw and bleeding. I wanted to throw those horrid little creatures back into the Gulf, not painstakingly fill a bucket with them—but filling a bucket meant earning money, so fill the buckets I did.

During the summer, I participated in a jobs program offered by the Gulf Oil Company. Just two of us from my school were given the opportunity to work for them, painting tanks and mowing the lawn—all in the blazing Louisiana summer sun. But the job paid well, and I was happy to have it. I didn't like the heat, but it was better than peeling those horrible shrimp! My younger siblings worked too. We all helped out at the school, waxing and buffing floors or cleaning classrooms. We worked hard, and we worked together. Everybody gave their money to Mama to buy food or to save. We all wanted out. We wanted to be free.

When my mother announced to me that she was planning a shopping trip to New Orleans, I was really excited. It had been a long time since we'd done this. I knew she had to work really hard to save any money, and I had great anticipation for the new clothes and shoes we would come home with. The two of us took the long bus ride into the city, and my excitement grew with each passing mile. But my mood began to change when we stopped for lunch and she explained how desperate our situation was. She was afraid my stepfather was going to kill her—and she'd no longer be able to provide for us or protect us from him. As she talked, the furrows in her brow deepened. Her shoulders were hunched from the weight of a burden heavier than any woman was meant to carry.

"Dorothy, I know I promised to buy you some new clothes,"

she began, "but, baby, we need to use that money to buy a car." She paused, searching my face to see if I understood. I blinked hard to hold back tears of disappointment. I felt selfish. I had bragged to my friends about shopping in the big city, and now I would come home with nothing—again. How tired I was of not having nice things! But I wanted to escape the abuse—I hated it. Even more than that, I wanted my mother to be free. I swallowed hard and shoved my disappointment down deep inside. I looked her in the eyes, and my selfish thoughts faded away. I loved her more in that moment than I ever had.

"It's time to escape!" I said. She breathed a long sigh, and her shoulders seemed to square up a bit.

"Yes, Dorothy," she smiled, "it is time for us to be free." She lifted her chin and closed her eyes, and I knew she was praying.

We came home from New Orleans without any new clothes, but we now had a car. All the way home, I wondered how my stepfather would react. I wasn't sure it mattered that much—he was going to be abusive no matter what my mother did, so why not put a plan in place to get free once and for all? I knew Mama was anxious too. She was quiet during the whole ride home. At the same time, there was a determined look in her eyes. She gripped the steering wheel of that car like her life depended on it. She could taste freedom. I sensed she was making plans, thinking things through. Every now and then, she wiped away a tear, looked over at me, and smiled.

Buying the car was the right choice. I knew it was. But it was only one step in the plan, and it had taken all of our savings. We couldn't escape until we had some money to run with. We needed enough cash to find a place to live and to survive until my mother could secure a new job.

Throughout this difficult season, one of my teachers was particularly kind to me. Miss Garlington knew about the violence at home and the emotional roller coaster I lived on. She often encouraged me, calmed me down, redirected my energy into positive pursuits, and challenged me to dream of a better future. Her presence in my life was a bright beacon in a dark sea. So when she accepted a teaching position 350 miles away in Monroe, I was devastated. *How could she leave? She was the one person in my life who seemed to really understand how awful it all was.*

As the day for her departure approached, I panicked. But Miss Garlington held out hope to me. On her last day, she pulled me aside and said, "After I get settled, maybe I can help you all move to Monroe and get away from your stepfather. I could help your mother find a job." My heart soared! Of course she would help us. Surely, this was our answer to prayer. How long had I asked God for an escape—and here it was! Miss Garlington wouldn't let me down. Now I just needed to convince Mother that the time was right.

I was convinced the pieces of our plan were falling into place. I had the promise from Miss Garlington tucked in my pocket, and we had a car. With help from friends, Mother was even learning to read and write, and her confidence was growing. All we needed now was enough money to run with. However, even with all these little steps moving us in the right direction, we were still trapped. The abuse worsened. My stepfather stopped contributing money to the household altogether, and my mother saved every possible dime for our great escape. We ate free lunches at school, and in the afternoon we drank milk from leftover school milk cartons and ate mayonnaise sandwiches. For the first time in my life, I realized we lived in poverty, and I felt ashamed.

My older brother Gary was now sixteen, and his boyhood anger had developed into full-grown hate. One night, he jumped on my stepfather, hit him hard, and then ran away. The next day, my stepfather tried to run over him with his truck. Just in time, my brother dropped to the ground and rolled beneath our trailer. The brakes grabbed and the tires locked, throwing a huge cloud of dust as the truck stopped mere inches from our mobile home. If Gary hadn't rolled under the trailer, I was certain my stepfather would have killed him.

This marked a turning point in our family dynamics. From that moment on, the abuse began to filter down to the six children. My stepfather still reserved a special kind of meanness for just my mother, but his rage was no longer confined only to her.

CHAPTER 4

Freedom

Freedom means you are unobstructed
in living your life as you choose. Anything
less is a form of slavery.

Wayne Dyer

M ama!" I cried. Tears were streaming down my cheeks.
I was both frightened and angry. "Mama!" I said again,
louder. I stroked her forehead and cheeks with a cool, damp
cloth. She was so still. After another beating by my stepfather,
she'd had a severe seizure and lost consciousness.

I looked down at her face and thought how beautiful she
was, even with the bruises. I loved her deeply. What if this was
her last beating? What if she didn't wake up? I shook her gently,
praying she would open her eyes and look at me.

"Mama," I said, softly this time. One of my tears splashed
on her cheek, and her eyes fluttered open. She grimaced in pain
and looked around in confusion. She felt so small lying there
in my arms.

"We must leave, Mama," I urged, my mind racing with fear.
"Please?" I begged. "Let's just get in the car and go!"

Her eyes held mine for a moment, and I could see she was
seriously considering it. "Please, Mama!" I said again. "We can
go to Monroe. Miss Garlington promised she would help us.
She's been waiting for us to come. Let's just go!"

And go we did.

It was Christmas break. Seven of us packed everything we
could fit into the car and then squeezed ourselves in. Anxiety
kept us all quiet at first, each of us lost in our own thoughts.
*Would we ever return? What would my stepfather do when he found
out? Would he follow us? Where were we going? What about our*

friends? Would we see them again? Would Mother be okay? Where would we live? What about school?

The farther away we drove, the more our mood lightened. Freedom! We could taste it. Someone told a joke, and we all laughed, releasing the tension. We sang a Christmas carol, and suddenly our anxiety gave way to a sense of adventure. Relief swept over us, and there was no looking back. *We had done it!* I resisted the urge to let out a yell, and I secretly wished I could see the look on my stepfather's face when he came home in the wee hours of the morning screaming for his supper and found us all gone!

We stayed a few nights in New Orleans, first with my great-grandmother and then with a great-aunt, but both homes were small — and seven extra people would have been difficult to accommodate no matter what size the home. My mother didn't want to be a burden, so after we woke up, we tidied everything up and stayed outside during the day. We had to find activities to keep all the children busy, and this proved increasingly difficult to do. Staying with relatives was not the answer.

After a few days, my mother decided the only thing to do was to head for Monroe and find Miss Garlington. We had no idea where she lived or how she might help us, but we were determined to find a better life, so we packed up again, piled into our Chevrolet Impala, and headed for Monroe. On the trip there, my mother began to feel ill. By the time we arrived, she was very sick. We checked into a motel, but Mother had caught the flu and was too ill to look for work.

We looked up Miss Garlington's telephone number, and I called her. I was excited to hear her voice on the other end of the line, and I almost shouted that we were at last here in Monroe. We had come just as she had suggested! I expected her to be overjoyed to hear from me, and I was sure she would come right over to rescue us. However, the response on the end of the line was far from the joyful one I anticipated. She sounded shocked and clearly taken off guard. When I told her my mother was ill, instead of rushing in to assist, Miss Garlington was hesitant to help. In the end, she proved to be no help at all.

I was crushed. Miss Garlington had promised to help us escape. She had always been a mentor to me, and I trusted her. Now, when I needed her most, she did not make good on her word. I never felt more alone than I did in that motel room. My heart was broken, and I felt betrayed. I was angry and frightened and confused—and determined not to go back to my stepfather.

Mother grew sicker and sicker, but we couldn't afford a doctor, much less an extended stay in a motel. Without Miss Garlington's assistance, we didn't have many options. Disheartened, we packed everything back into the Impala and headed back toward New Orleans.

This time, there were no jokes or songs or laughter. The mood in the car was subdued. My mood was blackest of all. I had convinced Mother to go to Monroe, and I had let her down—I had let the whole family down. My hope vanished like a mirage in the desert, and something inside me broke. Hot, angry tears streamed from my eyes. *How could Miss Garlington do this? What would we do now?* Mother tried to comfort me. She told me that God would take care of us and that it wasn't Miss Garlington's fault.

We made our way back to New Orleans, not knowing how we would survive. We checked into another motel, our money all but gone. Sick but determined, my mother called Ms. Terry, a good friend from the Church of Christ back home. She told her we were out of money and needed to find a place to stay in New Orleans. Ms. Terry called Elysian Fields Church of Christ in New Orleans to share our plight.

These beautiful people came out right away to see us. A dear woman who introduced herself as Sister Rew immediately set things into motion. She found us a place to live near my great-grandmother's house and somehow gathered necessities to help us through. All six of us were enrolled in school, though now instead of attending the same school together, as we had in Buras, we had to be in three different schools, and I had to go alone.

Each morning, I walked Helaine, John, and Leslie to their school and then walked about nine more miles to my school. My mother resumed her job as a custodian and carpooled for the seventy-five-minute commute back to Buras. This required her to rise before 5:00 a.m. each day to catch her ride by 5:30. The long commute was difficult, and she still suffered from seizures and headaches. Her absence meant I had more responsibility to care for my younger siblings. We were far away from my aunts and our community of family and friends, which meant I was on my own when Mother was gone. And things here were different — fast-paced and dangerous. We no longer suffered abuse, but we couldn't exactly say things were good.

In time, I made friends. Most of them walked halfway to school and then caught public transportation for the rest of the way. I didn't have any money, so I couldn't afford to ride with them. I pretended I liked the exercise, and I was so athletic that no one seemed to question my motives.

Many of my friends skipped school and got into trouble hanging around Bourbon Street. Sometimes these friends offered me rides, but I knew better than to accept. I was keenly aware of the price my mother had paid for our escape and what she had sacrificed for our safety. I admired her bravery, and I couldn't bear the thought of disappointing her or wasting her sacrifice. She wanted us to have a better life. She wanted me to get an education and have better choices. I wouldn't have traded that for anything.

I often walked to the corner grocery store to purchase scraps of meat and other necessities. A nice boy my age worked there, and we occasionally struck up a conversation. Like others, he too offered to drive me to school, but I declined. When I said no, he decided he would walk with me and maybe then we could work our way up to riding in his car. I did like him, but I wasn't ready to trust again. Miss Garlington's betrayal was still too fresh in my mind. Even this kind gesture felt like pressure I wasn't ready to deal with.

When the spring semester ended, I was fifteen and had just completed my sophomore year of high school. We had made our escape and were surviving, but my mother's health worsened. She could no longer continue the long commute back and forth to Buras each day. And she was increasingly concerned about how much time we spent alone and fending for ourselves. Eventually, she secured a job at a hotel in downtown New Orleans and worked another part-time job to make ends meet. But her body never really recovered from the abuse she had suffered, and working long hours with so little rest continued to take a toll. Mother got sick again, and the precarious balance of our lives once more spun out of control.

CHAPTER 5

Back to Buras

Every tyrant who has lived
has believed in freedom for himself.

Elbert Hubbard

My mother called me into her room and shut the door.

"Dorothy," she said, her voice soft and mellow, "I know how hard you worked so we could leave. I don't think I ever could have done it without you." She paused to gather her thoughts, and I felt my stomach tighten. "I am so very proud of you. I want all my children to have the chance for a better life."

"You're so smart," she continued. "I know you can be something and make something of yourself. You are almost a grown woman." Her voice trailed away, and for a moment her thoughts drifted to something far away.

She lifted my chin and smoothed my hair with a gesture so gentle you would have thought I was a newborn baby, not a young woman about to enter her junior year of high school. My heart was racing. I looked into her eyes, searching for a clue about where she was going with this conversation. Before she even said the words, I knew they were coming.

"We can't stay here in New Orleans anymore," she said. "We need to go back home."

Silence.

I held my breath. I wasn't sure what to feel. Waves of emotion rolled over me like the crazy pattern of the waves in the Gulf before an approaching storm. My mind raced. *Home?* I thought. *Is she crazy? He'll kill us!* I was holding a handkerchief in my hands, and I twisted it round and round, trying to settle my mind and emotions.

"What is the plan?" I finally asked, breaking the silence. "When do you want to go? What do you need me to do?"

In the next few minutes, my mother rattled off details like a military general. I could tell she had been thinking this through for some time and there would be no changing her mind. She kept assuring all of us that things would be different. She was sure my stepfather would be so happy to have us home that he wouldn't want to drink anymore. We were less enthusiastic, but as we packed and talked about seeing our aunts and cousins again, the mood in our little place brightened. Life in New Orleans had been hard, and it was easy to believe that going home might be the best thing after all.

Mother was right. Lester was really glad to see us. I don't know what he and Mother talked about, but he was eager for us to move back into the trailer, and he was genuinely helpful getting us settled in.

For the first few months, it seemed like a dream. There were lots of big family dinners, and it was lovely to see my aunts and laugh with my cousins again. Things felt familiar and safe and normal. The people at our church were overjoyed at our return and made us feel welcome. My mother got her old job back. She looked younger, and she smiled more often. My stepfather seemed to want this to work as well. He had missed us. I know he loved my mother, and he seemed to love us too. *Maybe this would work out after all!*

My stepfather and I even had some good times together. He decided it was time for me to learn how to drive. We spent many hours together as he taught me how to steer and use the gas pedal and the brake. It was the most fun I had ever had with him. During my driving lessons, I imagined this was what normal dads did with their daughters. Things really were different. Everything was going to be okay—this time for good.

But it wasn't for good. A few weeks later, I awoke to a crash in the kitchen. It was 3:30 a.m., and an angry voice had shattered the stillness of the night. There were harsh words — something about my mother being worthless and why didn't she have something decent ready for him to eat. I squeezed my eyes shut, hoping this was a bad dream. Then another crash, and a cabinet door slammed shut. My mother was crying now. I couldn't actually hear her, but I knew she was crying. The nightmare had returned.

I heard the unmistakable sound of a hand striking flesh and felt sick to my stomach. I felt as though a giant hand were pressing me into my mattress. I couldn't breathe. I couldn't move. I was bound as surely as if shackles were locked tightly around my arms and legs. "God!" I shouted. Another slap. "Jesus!" I cried. I sobbed until my pillow was wet with tears. "Please," I whispered. I was gripped by fear and anger. I felt like I was choking. "Please, God …" is all I could manage to say.

In the morning, I got up for school and headed to the kitchen. There was no trace of the fight. My mother had cleaned everything up like it never even happened. We were all quiet — deathly quiet. Even the birds were silent. No one dared to speak. Mother fixed breakfast without a word, but no one had any appetite. "Eat, children," she commanded, but there was no energy in her words. We dutifully took a bite or two, and one by one we slipped out for school.

The fairy tale had ended. The routine of drunken violence returned as though nothing had ever interrupted it.

Located on our property, sitting parallel to our trailer, was an even smaller, vacant two-bedroom trailer. One day after school, Mother announced we were moving over there. It was crazy. All seven of us were going to move into that tiny space and leave the larger trailer for my stepfather. It didn't make any sense, but none of us even bothered to ask my mother why he didn't move out instead. We simply packed our clothes and bedding and walked across the yard to our new home.

My mother continued to cook, clean, and do laundry for my stepfather. They stayed married, but lived in separate trailers. Sometimes he came home drunk in the middle of the night and banged on our door, screaming for my mother to come outside. Those were terrible nights. We kept the door locked and huddled in the dark, waiting for the alcohol to make him sleepy so he would leave. Sometimes he cried or begged or apologized, and my mother cried too. Even though he was terrible, she loved him.

Eventually, my older brother Gary couldn't take it anymore. He left school and got a job. Before long, he was married and determined to have a better life, or at least a new one. The physical abuse was less now that we lived in a separate trailer, but the emotional and verbal abuse was disruptive and damaging. Long after the yelling stopped, I could still hear it in my head.

~~

I often felt like I lived two separate lives. One life was at home — and everything there was mechanical. I did chores, cooked food, washed clothes, took care of my brothers and sisters, and worried about my mother. I felt trapped. I loved my family but hated how we lived. But at school, things were different. There, I was alive. I made choices for myself, and people respected me.

Sports continued to be my passion. When I was competing, I felt powerful and in control. I was confident. I was safe. I was strong. Volleyball, basketball, softball, track — if there was a team, I was on it. I studied as hard as I practiced sports, and

I got good grades. I ran for student council and won. I was involved in the school's drama department and loved acting in plays. Though our school did not have an official debate team, there were many opportunities for public speaking and recitations. I eagerly looked forward to participating in these and enjoyed traveling to competitions. One of my favorites was called "Girls State," where we traveled to the state capitol to give speeches, competing for political positions. You had to know politics, have a platform, and be able to give a new speech for each level of advancement. I made it all the way to secretary of state. It was such fun!

I began to think about college and dream of bigger and brighter things. I didn't really have any role models, because not many of the women in my family had graduated from high school, much less even considered going to college. There were times I felt lost and on my own, but I was determined nevertheless.

During my senior year, one of my teammates and I qualified for state finals in track. I was so excited! This meant a trip to Baton Rouge and a chance to compete in front of college scouts who might offer a scholarship. I trained hard. Two teachers were driving us to the competition. As we started out, the weather suddenly turned very bad. It was raining cats and dogs, and it was hard to see the road ahead. One of the teachers leaned over the seat and asked, "Do you girls really want to go to this meet?" I just stared at her and didn't know what to say. *Of course I want to go to the meet!* I thought. I had been training and preparing and planning for it for weeks. My teammate laughed and said, "Not really, why?" Just like that, they headed for Bourbon Street in New Orleans — the competition in Baton Rouge was no longer on the agenda. They pulled the car into Pat O'Brien's and shut down the engine. I sat there in disbelief.

I wanted to say something, but nothing came out of my mouth. I followed them inside, but my feet felt like lead.

The two teachers had a cocktail, and another, and then they ordered one for my friend. I was miserable and wanted to leave. I couldn't help but think of Miss Garlington—and all those old feelings of betrayal began to surface. *Why do people act this way?* I decided I was going to talk to the principal when we returned. I scripted the whole conversation in my mind as I sat there listening to them laugh. But I never followed through on it. The teachers told the school administrator that the weather was too bad to make it to Baton Rouge and had forced us to turn back. Of course, no mention was ever made of the detour and the drinking. Once again, my trust was broken.

✧

Graduation! I was the first in my family—first daughter, first granddaughter, and first niece to ever graduate from high school, and my family celebrated in grand style. They were so supportive and we had a giant celebration. I really did feel special.

I had no sense of what college to attend, but when I was offered a partial academic scholarship to the University of Southwestern Louisiana (which later became the University of Louisiana at Lafayette), it made the decision an easy one. That scholarship, combined with a Pell Grant, meant I could go to college. Once again, my hopes soared! I could hardly wait for fall to come.

The college prepared a list of items that incoming freshmen needed. It included everything from bedding and an iron to toiletries and shower shoes. My mother guarded that list like it was a priceless historical document. Little by little, one by one, we purchased every single item on the list. She was determined I would have everything I needed to get an education.

"You're going to get a good education, Dorothy," she would say. "Now, don't you be distracted by them boys. What they want won't help you open up your own business anyhow." I can still hear her voice rambling off thoughts and advice as she washed dishes or hulled peas. "You're a strong leader, Dorothy Johnson. You've got a good head on your shoulders. You make sure you find a good church and stay in it! You're gonna be somebody. Oooooh, I'm so proud of you!"

That summer flew by. I could hardly wait to start my first semester in college. My life, I felt sure, was finally about to begin.

PART 2

College and Young Adulthood

CHAPTER 6

College

College is a catalyst for change, but change
only comes to those willing to embrace it.

J. Rowan Samson

I pinched myself. *Is this real? Am I actually here — in my very own dorm room, away from home, a college girl?*

It was real. I felt myself smiling, and I looked around, surveying my new room with satisfaction.

Before my enrollment, my mother made sure we visited several nearby churches that I could attend regularly. At each one, she fired off a list of questions to the minister:

- "Does your church have a program for college students?"
- "Do you provide transportation for them?"
- "How often can you pick up my daughter so she can be involved in your church?"
- "Do you have a weekday service?"
- "What kinds of activities are scheduled for students?"

And on and on she went. She totally overwhelmed one poor little minister. He couldn't answer one question before my mother asked him two more. He just shook or nodded his head a lot and then showed us the door as fast as he could! One minister, however, had answers for every single one of my mother's questions, and I could tell she was pleased. Whether I liked the place or not, I knew this was the church I would attend. Once Keeby set her mind on something, there was little point in arguing.

I settled easily into the dormitory but was a little nervous about having a roommate I didn't know. I was used to living in close quarters but had always been with family—lots of family. Suddenly, they seemed very far away, and I was afraid. I felt responsible for them, and I was worried about not being there to help with chores and earning money. So much was at stake. My whole family was counting on me to be a success, and I did not want to let them down.

As I was enrolling in classes, I discovered the school had a volleyball team. That was it! I would try out for the team. I didn't even hesitate. I knew sports. I was alive on a court, and there was no place that felt more like home to me. My talent soon caught the coach's eye. She was a good coach, and under her leadership I grew stronger as an athlete. She told me that if I did well that season, there was a strong possibility of a scholarship for next year. That was all I needed to hear. I worked harder than ever and was disciplined in my practice regimen, diet, and studies. I knew this was an answer to prayer.

The campus minister my mother had interviewed also watched me with interest. The church wanted to launch a college ministry, but they needed a student who lived on campus to lead it. I was their girl. The minister and his wife approached me cautiously, testing the waters to see if I was open to accepting the responsibility. There it was again—responsibility. People always relied on me to get the job done, to sacrifice, to never let them down. I had just completed the first week of my first semester, and all I wanted was to concentrate on my studies and on volleyball. I wasn't sure I wanted the added duties of running a campus ministry. I didn't feel qualified. Plus, I had long-term goals and was focused on those. I was concerned that leading a ministry might negatively impact my grades and my commitment to the volleyball team.

I'm not sure how it happened, but before long, I was meeting with a group in the student center a few times a week. I never formally agreed to anything, but the meetings began to fill my calendar. New people showed up at almost every gathering. Some were just trying to connect and make friends, but many had special needs and looked to me to help them solve their problems. It was a dilemma for me. I wanted to make friends too, and there was a level of fulfillment in helping others, but my classes were demanding, and I had volleyball practice twice a day, six days a week. I was tired and overwhelmed. I could feel the weight of my family's expectations, my coach's expectations, and my own expectations to excel in my classes—and now there was the added pressure to meet the needs of a growing campus ministry. It was too much.

Just three short weeks into the semester, I was questioning everything. *Am I trying to please God or people? Why am I here? Is this the right college? What's my purpose? How am I going to do all this? Did they ask me to lead because I'm capable, or just available? Is this really my calling?* Joy left me. Now it was duty, not desire, that drove me out of bed each day. I felt like a robot. I was going through the motions and meeting expectations, but nothing inside felt alive.

It was Wednesday night, and I had just finished the second volleyball practice for the day. I had been in classes all day, and I hadn't eaten. I was irritable and slipped into complaining. I did that more and more. Even when I didn't complain out loud, I complained in my head. I felt sorry for myself, and I was frustrated with people around me who didn't work as hard as I did. They seemed lazy to me. The church van was on its way to pick me up, but I was too exhausted and miserable to care. I looked at my watch—yikes! I let out a loud huff, then quickly showered and somehow managed to catch the van. I'm glad I did.

That night began like most others, students socializing with each other. There was the familiar buzz of conversation that rose and fell with laughter and stories. I was just beginning to relax enough to engage with people when an authoritative voice cut through the chatter.

"Young men and women," the voice said, "I'm telling you to seek first his kingdom and his righteousness, then all the other things you need will be given to you."

It was the minister speaking the words, but it was God who planted them in my heart. Something stirred down deep in my soul. I felt warm inside, and I smiled. Was that joy I felt returning? "Seek God *first*," the minister said, "and then all these things shall be given unto you." Simple. From that moment on, I sought to put God first, and the pressure of obligations and expectations seemed to vanish. I was as busy as ever, but now I felt alive. The robot was gone for good. I had a purpose, and every day was new and amazing.

When Thanksgiving came, I went home feeling so grown-up. It had only been a few months, but it seemed like a year had passed since I left Buras. I was different on the inside. My perspective had changed, and going home was hard. But I was happy to see everyone, and you haven't had Thanksgiving dinner until you've had one Louisiana style! It was the best food I had ever eaten—how I had missed this!

My aunts couldn't hear enough about my dormitory and my roommate. They wanted to know all about my classes and playing for the team, and my mother was *so* pleased that I had become deeply involved with the church's campus ministry. I felt important. Everyone seemed genuinely interested in all the details of my college life, and I was overwhelmed by their attention. The weekend seemed like a brief moment, and all too soon it was time to return to school.

My stepfather drove for the three-hour ride back to campus. It was a little awkward. We began the trip in silence and kept to random, superficial topics for at least half the journey. Finally, without taking his eyes from the road, he said, "I don't mean to hurt her." I felt a catch in my throat. "I want to be a better person," he continued. "I don't know why I can't stop drinking and gambling. I just can't help it." He grew quiet again, and I wasn't sure what to say.

"I don't want to smoke either," he said after we had passed a few miles in silence. "You believe me, don't you, Dorothy? You have always been such a good girl — like your mother ..." His voice trailed off.

"Just stop drinking," I heard myself say, surprised at my own courage. "You can be so kind," I said. "I remember all the times you gave me money for sports and school activities, and you used to come to my softball games. Why can't you just be that person?"

"I wish I could," he sighed, and the silence returned.

Back at school, I immersed myself in the campus ministry. I hosted Bible studies and planned activities, all the while drawing in more and more people to meet Jesus. I looked forward to each opportunity and found myself inviting people daily. Within a few weeks, attendance had grown significantly. I was planting spiritual seeds and seeing fruit so quickly that it was exhilarating. I was excited, and my enthusiasm was contagious. I felt like a bright light had been turned on inside of me, and people were attracted to the warm glow.

⌇

There he was: "Kenny J." I had met him before Thanksgiving. He was handsome! I gave him a flyer and invited him to Bible study, and he came! I introduced him to the campus minister, and before long, Kenny accepted Christ as his Savior. Kenny was a persuasive communicator, and when he shared his testimony about accepting Jesus with the group, my heart filled to the brim. By the end of that first semester, we were head over heels in love.

At spring break, I took Kenny home to meet my family, and they all fell in love with him too. He fit right in, and I found myself beginning to trust him. I shared things with him I had never told anyone else. I told him about how abusive our lives had been as I was growing up and how scared and alone I had felt. Kenny shared his own challenges with me, and this drew us even closer together.

The time I spent with Kenny was magical. He loved God with all his heart. We spent lots of time together — talking, praying, studying the Word, and just being close. Our feelings for each other intensified, and it was the best time in my life.

When we returned to school in the fall, Kenny was a senior and already looking ahead to his future. When he began to talk of marriage, I found myself suddenly shy. I wasn't ready for that kind of commitment. I was still bruised from my past and from the betrayal I had experienced time and again. I wanted to give myself completely to Kenny, but part of me held back. I was deeply in love but not ready to commit.

"Seek first his kingdom" was etched on my heart. *How can I seek God if I am so involved in a relationship?* I thought to myself. I was starting my second year of college. I was back on a volleyball scholarship and had plans to play for the next three years. *What about my family?* I promised my mother I would finish school and be the first college graduate in the family. *What about the ministry?* People were coming to know Christ because of my involvement. *If I marry Kenny, what will happen to those people?* I fought with myself. One day, I could imagine leaving school to join Kenny in "happily ever after" wedded bliss. The next day, I was certain I had to focus on my goals or

I would always be filled with regret that would ultimately spoil my marriage.

Up and down I went, riding on an emotional roller coaster. Beneath it all was the legacy of my troubled childhood. I was determined that what happened to my mother would never happen to me. I wanted to be able to survive on my own—to be independent, well educated, and strong. Although I wasn't willing or able to acknowledge it, I was also afraid of yet another betrayal. This fear had built a self-protective fortress around my heart. No one could come in, and I couldn't come out. Fear imprisoned the part of me that wanted to love and trust another human being. I didn't realize it, but the prison was there as surely as if there were real iron bars and a lock encasing my heart.

During this time, my auntie Dee Dee wrote me letters, encouraging me to stay in school and finish my degree—there would be time for marriage later. Years ago, she had made plans to finish high school and then go to college, but instead she got married and moved away with her husband, Uncle Bubbie, who worked for the government. The responsibilities of being a wife and mother complicated things, and it was many years before she had the opportunity to return to school for her bachelor's degree. She spoke from personal experience about the limitations I would experience without that cherished college degree. I clung to her words as a source of encouragement and guidance. I was thankful for her wisdom, and this helped me to realize God had a plan for my life. I was thoroughly convinced that scholarships were his provision for my education. *Why would he have provided the money for me to go to school if I wasn't supposed to finish?* It would be wrong of me to waste this opportunity. I also thought about my siblings—I didn't want to be a dropout they couldn't look up to. Troubled by my past, absorbed in my present, and confused about my future, I pulled back from Kenny.

My relationship with Kenny had made me the envy of many girls in our campus fellowship. Kenny was a fine catch—handsome, well built, patient, well-spoken, kind, and sincerely good. Every young woman in our ministry wanted Kenny, but I was the lucky one he chose. Throughout our relationship, I was proud to be with him, and I felt special that he wanted to be with me.

But as Kenny's senior year progressed and he became increasingly insistent about wanting deeper commitment and more of my time, I had less time to give. In addition to the campus ministry, I was focused on my studies and took my position with the volleyball team very seriously. I needed time to keep my grades up and perform well on the team. As a result, we spent much less time together, and our relationship grew shaky.

I truly wanted to be Kenny's wife. I believed he was the man God had for me. I even dreamed about it, but I also firmly believed it had to be after college. Then and only then could I allow myself to become an adoring and wonderful wife. Looking back, I know that fear played a much larger role in my reluctance to commit than I realized at the time. I had known the harshness of anger and abuse. I had felt the sting of betrayal by people I loved and trusted—and I still suffered from that pain. I wasn't willing to hand Kenny an opportunity to hurt me in that way. I pursued my goals and pushed him farther and farther away until one day, he stopped trying to get close.

Kenny moved on.

CHAPTER 7

Home away from Home

It is not so much our friends' help that
helps us as the confidence of their help.

Epicurus

I knew Kenny was seeing someone else. We never officially broke up, but we drifted apart until I knew the relationship had died. I knew he would bring his new girl to a meeting one day, and I dreaded it. Even though I genuinely wished him the best and wanted him to be happy, the thought of seeing him happy with someone else was painful. *Oh, if only he was willing to wait!*

When my reluctance to commit became evident, one girl in the group who had never been fond of me (at least in my mind) quickly encouraged Kenny to move on. "Pursuing Dot is a waste of time," she told him. She introduced him to a friend of hers and encouraged him to ask her out. Real or imagined, it seemed as though she celebrated my loss—perhaps I had gotten what I deserved. Each time I went to a meeting, I could feel her eyes on me and imagine what she whispered to others: "Good for him!" "It's about time he moved on!" I wanted to escape.

The dreaded day finally came. He brought her to a meeting, and I was hurt. The old feelings of betrayal surfaced, and it was difficult to push them aside and focus on God and my goals. A wrestling match was taking place inside my soul. I argued with myself, gave myself pep talks, and sometimes cried out to God in desperation. I questioned if I had done the right thing in rejecting Kenny's offer for a future together, and I struggled to keep my focus on my studies.

To further complicate matters, our campus ministry group naturally fostered deep relationships, and people began pairing off. Fifteen couples who met in our group ultimately went all the way to the altar. I was truly happy for each and every one of them, but something inside me felt empty and hollow. *Will I ever know that kind of happiness? Will I ever trust someone enough to walk down the aisle? Will he treat me well? Will he hurt me?* These thoughts tormented me in moments of quietness, and I turned them over to God, trusting him to bring me peace.

Kenny was very kind to me during this time, and he placed some distance between us before involving his new girlfriend in campus ministry. I appreciated his sensitivity, but just being in the same room with this girl was enough to drive me to distraction. The disappointment in my soul was intense. I felt neglected as I never had before and had to grapple with my emotions privately so I could find the strength and maturity to be gracious and kindhearted in social situations.

Unwilling to lose face or let anyone know how deeply hurt I was, I continued to study with the group and participate in all the activities. I even encouraged other members of the group to reach out to Kenny's new girlfriend and love her. After all, that's what Christ would have done, and I genuinely wanted to be a follower of Christ. I was quick to assure anyone who expressed concern for me that I was fine. With a forced but convincing smile, I explained that the breakup with Kenny was not his fault—someone else was able to give him what he needed now, and I wasn't that person. He deserved to be happy.

Many times I was tempted to go to Kenny, apologize, and tell him how I really felt—that I loved and needed him. When I imagined the scene in my mind, it always ended with him asking me to marry him (again), but this time I would look into his eyes and say, "Yes, Kenny!" Sometimes I even picked up the phone, but then I always put it back down again. I just couldn't bring myself to do it. It would be a lie. I wasn't ready to love like that—or to be loved like that.

Something on the inside of me was deeply wounded. I had never shared my traumatic childhood with anyone other than Kenny, so no one knew the depth of fear and inability to trust I experienced. I was simply not capable of accepting Kenny's goodness, kindness, and genuine love for me. My emotional defenses were fortress strong, and I felt powerless to tear them down and let him inside.

The remainder of my sophomore and junior years was difficult and lonely. However, it was during this time that I met Wayne and Jane Nance through a "home away from home" program at our church. Mrs. Nance became my mentor, and oh, what divine providence it was that brought her into my life! She pointed out the good she saw in me and challenged me to reach for God's best in every area of my life. She helped me see my failures as stepping-stones to success and use these for growth and development, not as anchors to weigh me down. She encouraged me to honor Christ with all my actions and to seek his guidance in every decision. I wanted to be like her, and in a very short time I had grown remarkably close to her.

Her wisdom and gentleness disarmed me. I soon found myself venting my closely guarded fears and feelings. My defenses fell away, and I felt safe enough to share my pain. Her calm demeanor and willingness to listen wrapped around me like a warm blanket. She gently navigated the storms in my soul and helped me chart a course into calm waters—a place where God's love was all-encompassing. It was the first time I experienced inner healing, and I knew I was on my way to a new beginning.

But then it happened again—another loss. After just six

weeks of spending time with Mrs. Nance, her husband, Wayne, received a job transfer that required a move to Houston. I was devastated.

"Why, God?" I cried. The same sinking feeling I experienced when Miss Garlington told me she was moving away came back. After I had allowed myself to trust Mrs. Nance by sharing all the details of my childhood, the intimate details of my relationship with Kenny, and my vulnerable feelings about the breakup, she was leaving. I had just begun the process of healing and was beginning to hope I might bring closure to these painful events and start anew when everything abruptly halted. Just as the shame, fear, and feelings of unworthiness had started to melt away, they threatened to return like a flood and drown me in their wake.

How could this happen to me—again? What was wrong with me?

The day the Nances left, I was so overcome with emotion that I could not even go to send them off. I wept bitterly, but there was no solace in my tears. Once again, a shoulder I trusted enough to cry on had disappeared, and I was left to cry alone—silent tears.

I was certain I would never be able to trust again.

CHAPTER 8

Gunshot and Grace

Above all the grace and the gifts
that Christ gives to his beloved
is that of overcoming self.

Francis of Assisi

It was the spring of 1983, and I was in my senior year of college. Things were looking up! It had been a successful volleyball season, and even in the off-season I remained disciplined in physical conditioning. I was strong and healthy and in the best shape of my life. I was over Kenny and once again happy in my involvement in the campus ministry. I was going to graduate that December with a degree in sociology and business. I was proud of what I had achieved and excited about the future.

One April morning, I was sitting in my dorm room studying when I received an unexpected call from my volleyball coach telling me she was on her way over. *Had something happened at home? Had something bad happened to my mother? Why else would Coach be coming?*

I began to pray earnestly, asking God for strength. I prayed that my mother was not dead. I feared that my stepfather had beaten her to death, and I suddenly felt guilty for being away from home. I told God I could handle anything but my mother being dead.

It seemed as though hours passed before my coach finally arrived, though it had been only a few minutes. When I answered the door, I saw she had brought several of my teammates. My heart sank, and I felt my knees shake. Adrenaline jolted through my body, and my thoughts spun out of control. Clearly this was bad news. I searched the faces of my teammates looking for a clue—everyone was visibly upset.

"What is it?" I asked. "Please? Is it my mama?"

My coach came inside, and we sat on the edge of my bed. She held my hand and slowly said, "Dot, your stepfather has been shot." I stared at her in disbelief.

"He's in the hospital in critical condition," she continued. I let out a sigh of relief.

"Oh, Mama," I whispered, tears streaming down my face. "Thank God ..." I'm sure my coach didn't understand my reaction—how could she? I had never told anyone on the team how my stepfather treated my mother.

"I need to go to her," I said as I stood up to pack. "Wait, I should call her—" and I looked around the room confused, as if I couldn't remember how to use a telephone.

One of my teammates helped me call home, and I was still crying tears of relief that my mother was not harmed when she answered. "Dorothy? Is that you?"

"Yes, Mama, it's me, Dorothy," I said. I was so happy to hear her voice.

"Baby, listen to me. You need to focus on your schoolwork," she said. "I'm alright." Ever practical, Keeby did not want my studies to suffer, even in the face of a crisis as big as this one.

"But, Mama ..." I interrupted.

"Listen to me, Dorothy Johnson," she continued. "You couldn't get in to see him right now even if you were here. He's in intensive care. Why don't you wait until the weekend? You can come then without missing any of your classes. I'm fine. Really."

"Who shot him?" I asked. "How did this happen? Where is he?" For a moment, I felt panic rise and thought to myself, *O God—Mama, you didn't pull the trigger did you? Was it self-defense? Did he hurt you?* I said none of this out loud, but she told me enough details that I realized with relief she hadn't been the one who shot him.

Since none of my friends had any idea about my background,

I couldn't really share any of the terrible things that were running through my mind. I was grateful for their concern, and several of them stayed for a while to make sure I was okay. But I was in turmoil, and part of me just wanted to be left alone.

I was deeply concerned for my mother. In spite of the horror he had put her through, I knew she genuinely cared about this man. No matter how he treated her or what awful things he said to her, she had continued to cook his meals, clean his trailer, wash his clothes, and pay his bills. That night, I eventually fell into a fitful sleep, praying that God would watch over my mother and help her through this new storm.

The next morning, my sister called, crying. "What is it?" I asked. "What's wrong?" I asked again, this time a bit more forcefully.

"It's Mama," she said, and the crying started again. "Dorothy, you've got to come home. Now!" This was too much. I sat down hard, dazed. "She's sick," my sister said through more tears. "She's in intensive care."

I stared at the receiver. *Did I hear her right? Mama!* The moment I hung up, fierce energy poured through my body. When I heard about my stepfather, my feet had turned to stone. Now, when I heard about my mother, it felt like fire was coursing through my veins. I hastily threw some clothes into a bag and sped home. I didn't even think about the consequences of missing class or practice. I didn't take time to notify anyone; I just knew I had to get home. *Home*, I thought. *Mama is my home. Without her there isn't any home.* The car couldn't go fast enough.

My mother had suffered a heart attack. I suppose the news of my stepfather was too much for her to bear. Now they were both in intensive care, two lives hanging in the balance. I felt like I had been kicked in the stomach. No matter how deeply I breathed, there just didn't seem to be enough air.

We received an outpouring of support from family, our church, and our friends. Everybody knew Keeby, and everyone seemed to want to help in some way. All across Plaquemines Parish, prayers were lifted on behalf of my mother and stepfather—earnest prayers—and God heard.

Within a few days, my mother showed remarkable signs of improvement and was moved out of the ICU into a regular room. We were a people who believed in miracles. We had seen them many times and trusted God for one now. He did not fail. Two weeks later, my stepfather was also moved out of intensive care and began his long road to recovery. This was truly a miracle—not just that he was alive, but that this experience finally brought him closer to Christ.

Police officers made several trips to the hospital, asking questions and investigating the details of the assault on my stepfather. They eventually filed a report, but they hadn't gotten to the bottom of the mystery of who had pulled the trigger. My stepfather offered up what little he remembered. He had been drinking and gambling at a nightclub he frequented. An argument broke out between him and another man. Things got heated until they were completely out of hand. A shot was fired, and he ended up with a bullet in his stomach. Rumors flew all around the county, and many speculated, but no one was able to name a plausible suspect, so no arrest was ever made. My stepfather had been too drunk to remember who he had the fight with.

My mother was just relieved he was alive and thanked God every day. It was amazing to watch how gentle she was with him and how attentive she was to his every need. Of course, we all were glad he was alive, but we were also partly glad he had tasted the consequences of irrational violence. I wrestled with my thoughts, but in time I chose to look at it as a chance for him to redeem himself and live a better life. God needed to shake him up to get his attention—and now he certainly had it.

People from the community came to visit my stepfather every day. Through acts of kindness, they demonstrated God's love for a man who had done very little to deserve such care. Some prayed with him or shared the gospel, giving him the opportunity to make a decision for Christ. He was encouraged to trust God to heal his body, to repent, and to turn his life around. God must have spared him for a reason and he best find out what that reason was. Slowly but surely, their kindness cracked his shell.

I visited him too. I knew it was the right thing to do. And I began to feel a burning desire for him to know Jesus. During my time in campus ministry, I had seen many students give their lives to Christ, and I wanted my stepfather to know him too.

When I was sitting with him one afternoon, a pleasant silence had filled the room. He looked over at me, and I saw kindness in his eyes. For the first time I could ever remember, he asked me about myself.

"How's school?" he asked. I was taken aback. He had never asked me a question like that before. I answered him cautiously, and though it was awkward at first, the more I talked, the easier it got.

"Tell me more about this campus ministry you're so involved in," he probed. I looked at him, searching for some sign of false concern on his face, but there was none. Once I started talking, I couldn't stop. It just flowed out. I told him all about my friends, the wonderful church I attended, and how families adopted students and mentored them and helped them discover their destiny. I told him about leading others to Christ and how God can change a life—any life, even his. I spoke of repentance and forgiveness and hope and healing, and my stepfather soaked up every word like a sponge. We lapsed into silence again after a time, and I thought the conversation was at an end. But it turned out there was more he wanted to know.

"Tell me," he said, "Tell me about what you want to do with your life, Dorothy."

I turned my head and looked at him in amazement. *Was this the same man who beat my mother? Was this the man who came home drunk in the middle of the night, demanding food and shouting obsceni-ties?* I looked at his face and felt God's love surround us both. God loved this man, and therefore so would I. In the weeks that followed, I continued to come back and visit every weekend.

As I drove back and forth from school to the hospital, I was flooded with memories of all the times my stepfather had driven me back to college after a visit at home. We usually went back on a Saturday after he'd had a chance to sleep it off and sober up. For the long, three-and-a-half-hour ride, it was just the two of us alone together. He often used the time to talk about himself and offer excuses for his behavior toward my mother. He always told me how sorry he was to have hurt her when he lost control. My stepfather claimed he wanted to stop drinking, but he repeatedly denied the needs of his family in favor of his desire to drink. I didn't hate him, even then. I felt sorry for him. He was trapped in a losing cycle, unable and unwilling to break free.

Yet here he was now, surviving a bullet to the stomach shot at point-blank range. Surely, God must have more for him. I was certain that if he gave his life to Christ, he could be free forever from the grip of alcohol and gambling. He could live a new and meaningful life. In fact, I could already see the signs that he was changing. During one of our visits, he told me how proud he was that I was going to earn my degree—and he wanted to be at my graduation! I was deeply moved.

To pass the time during our visits, we sometimes played a game to help strengthen his lungs. The hospital had given him a cylindrical device filled with hollow plastic balls, which had an attached tube with a mouthpiece. He was supposed to blow into the tube to see how high he could lift the plastic balls. The exertion helped to expand his lungs, preventing fluid from building up and causing additional health concerns. We took turns blowing into the device. When it was his turn, his face would contort so strangely that it made me laugh. Of course, the fact that he was competing against an athlete in top condition meant it was no contest, but it was a good time between us.

In the hospital, there was no chance for a drink, and he dried out completely for the first time in his adult life. I could see the impact that God's love was making on him. He was truly a changed man. He was growing warmer and friendlier by the day. I knew he would never be the same again, and I actually looked forward to our visits. I was hungry to be around him. I had never really known the love of a dad, and I wanted to experience it. The doctors had nothing but good news to report. In fact, his prognosis was so good that his release was planned for a few days later. I felt relaxed when I drove back to school, anticipating that our lives were finally about to change for the better.

It had been three days since my last visit to the hospital when my coach called to ask if she could stop by. She had been extremely supportive throughout the crises with my mother and stepfather, and I assumed she simply wanted to check on me. "Sure," I said easily, and I returned to my studies without any anxiety.

When she knocked, I opened the door with a big smile. But when I saw her, I instantly knew something was wrong. She had not come alone. Once again, she had assembled a group of team members, and by the look on everyone's faces, I knew the news was not good.

"Dorothy, honey, there is just no easy way to say this," she said. "Your stepfather is dead."

"How can that be?" I stammered. "I just saw him. He's getting better. He's supposed to go home today!" I shook my head in disbelief. "This can't be true," I said firmly. But it was true. My stepfather never got a chance to go home. He never had the opportunity to live out a changed life. Just when I had allowed myself to hope for a happy home for my mother, he was gone forever.

CHAPTER 9

Nothing Is Wasted

Life's challenges are not supposed to
paralyze you; they're supposed to help
you discover who you are.

Bernice Johnson Reagon

The night following the news of my stepfather's death, I lay in bed staring up at the ceiling. Hot tears spilled from the corners of my eyes and washed down my cheeks, making my pillow damp. I felt numb inside. *Why God?* I thought to myself. *Why didn't he get the chance to go home and live a new life like he was supposed to?*

Through a gentle whisper I felt the reassurance of the Holy Spirit. He told me that my stepfather did go home—just not to his home here on earth. When I heard the Holy Spirit speak to me so clearly, it changed my life. I realized God could use everything in my life—the good and the bad—to help me grow and mature. Nothing was wasted. Even the pain had purpose. I took great comfort in this.

In the days leading up to the memorial service, I made frequent calls to check in on my mother. She seemed more fragile now, and I remained deeply concerned for her health. I was sad to have lost my stepfather just when I was beginning to get to know him, but knowing that my mother was truly safe—totally free from danger—gave me great peace. I was relieved to know no one would ever abuse her again.

After my stepfather's home-going service, I spent some time with my family, but then I went back to school determined to put all the distractions behind me and finish my semester strong. But when I returned to school, there were distractions there too.

Kenny, the love of my life, was engaged to another woman. Danny and Theresa, the campus minister and his wife, had accepted a new ministry position and would soon move to Oklahoma. News of their leaving was a crushing blow. I had also finished my last year with the volleyball team, and my friends were beginning to marry and move off. It seemed as though everyone I had invested time in building a relationship with was moving on to do what God had planned for them. I wondered what God had planned for me.

When the spring semester ended, I went home for a short break before returning for summer school. My mother was still spending time and energy trying to deal with the death of my stepfather. Even though she wanted to put it behind her, the shooting was still under investigation, and my mother was being constantly dragged back into the ordeal. The stress was too much for her already failing health. She began to have frequent seizures, each one requiring more time to recover from than the previous one. I was powerless to change her situation, and as the time drew near for me to return to school, I had to lovingly place her in God's hands.

When I returned to school for the summer semester, life on campus was not the same as it had been. I was now the manager for the volleyball team, which was entirely different from simply being a team member. The church was in the process of hiring a new campus minister, so no one was leading the student ministry. Most of my friends had graduated in the spring, and moved on. I was not going to graduate until December, but I was just as eager to begin my postcollege life too. I was restless, lonely, and tired. And then came more bad news from home.

One evening, my mother called to tell me that Mary, my twenty-three-year-old stepsister, had been diagnosed with Hodgkin's disease and was in the hospital in Baton Rouge. Friends in my church knew some people in Baton Rouge and arranged a place for me to stay on weekends or whenever I needed to be there to support Mary and my mother.

I dreaded a return to the hospital. I was accustomed to being around young, vibrant, healthy people. I had come to hate hospitals. I felt nauseous and sometimes even vomited just being there. Walking the corridors brought unpleasant memories to the surface—memories of my stepfather's passing, fears of my mother's frailty, and now the uncertainty of my sister's future. In a hospital, I felt powerless, helpless, and frustrated. I desperately wanted to do more than offer up prayers and give words of encouragement. But prayers and words of encouragement were all I had to offer, so that's what I did.

Mary looked forward to my visits. She had developed a daily routine that included studying her Bible and reading daily devotionals. On the weekends, she wanted me to read aloud to her. Sometimes family members were present, and sometimes it was just the two of us. These were special times for me, and I was delighted to bring Mary some joy. Sharing God's Word with her created a deep bond between us.

Mary grew increasingly ill and showed no signs of improvement. It was so difficult for all of us watching her health deteriorate at such an alarming pace. As her body was failing, her relationship with God grew only stronger. Her primary concern was not for herself but for her children. She didn't want them to grow up without their mother. I looked into her eyes and felt such grief—she was so young. *Why God?* I thought to myself. *Why?*

Exactly two months and twenty-one days after my stepfather died, Mary joined him in heaven.

Once again our family plummeted into sadness and grief. Mary was gone. Death was now an overwhelming reality for me. It was my enemy. But even in the midst of loss, I found a deep appreciation for the gift of life. I was determined once again to make the very best of mine.

CHAPTER 10

New Beginnings

It's not the years in your life that count;
it is the life in your years.

Adlai Stevenson

Y ou're a *what?*" I asked.
        "I've become a Jehovah's Witness, baby," my mother
answered calmly.

"Why? When?" I managed to say. This was incomprehen-
sible. When we were younger, she wouldn't even allow us to
speak to a Jehovah's Witness for fear we would become confused. She loved telling people about Jesus, and her favorite
thing in the world was to lead someone to Christ. I couldn't
understand what had occurred to cause her to make this shift.
In fact, I later came to believe it was her zeal to witness and
evangelize that drew her to them.

Jehovah's Witnesses emphasize witnessing and still go
door-to-door to proselytize. Their emphasis on the equality
of all races and clean moral living were very appealing to my
mother. This I could understand, but there were other things
I most definitely could not understand — rejecting the symbol
of the cross, not believing in hell, and refusing to believe that
Jesus and the Holy Spirit are fully part of the Trinity. Beyond
the theological issues, Jehovah's Witnesses also abstained from
celebrating birthdays and traditional Christian holidays, which
further complicated things for me.

I loved my mother and respected her deeply, but I simply
could not agree with her new definition of faith and practice. The woman who had been my bedrock and given me a
strong foundation in the Bible — the woman who had led me
to Jesus — now accepted a version of salvation I could never

agree with. This too felt like a betrayal. Tensions between us mounted, and I did not want to move back home.

Dallas. That was the place for me. I had my degree in sociology and business neatly tucked under my jacket, and it was time to make my way in the world. My college roommate Sheila and I had been to Dallas several times on volleyball trips, and with each trip our desire to move there grew stronger. Dallas was a big city filled with excitement and opportunity. In Dallas we could expand our horizons, test our wings, and find our futures.

After graduation, Sheila went back home to find a job, gain some experience, and earn money to prepare for the move. I remained in Lafayette, rented a room from a delightful older woman named Ms. Rodgers, and found a job as an accountant at a wonderful company, Wm. S. Nacol Jewelry. I was gaining life experience, and I felt sturdy in my independence, but after a year I felt restless. I wasn't discontented, but I was eager for something more.

For months, I had been preparing to finally make the move to Dallas, and now it was time. New beginnings are exciting, but new beginnings require necessary endings—and these can be painful. Leaving my church family, school friends, and natural family was a difficult thing to do. I was a young, black woman leaving my support structure to forge my way in an unknown world. I had no job, no place to stay, few friends, and no real connections—just a dream, a spirit of adventure, and a belief that I was obeying God. I knew everything would work out.

When the time came to leave, I packed my car and began the five-hundred-mile drive to Dallas. After an overnight stay with friends in Houston, I finally arrived in Dallas—my new home. I immediately met up with Sheila, and we had a joyful reunion. She had been living in Dallas for six months, and her lease would soon expire. We had a ten-day window for me to find a job and for us to find a suitable apartment to share. That night, I asked the Lord to bless me with a good job to begin my career. Before going to bed, I checked the newspaper and mapped out several places to seek work the next day.

At the first place I interviewed, I was asked to return later that day for a second interview. That was a good sign. When I returned in the afternoon, the interview went so well that I knew beyond a shadow of doubt I would be offered the job. I was amazed at how quickly God had answered my prayer. Amazed, yes; surprised, no. I trusted God.

They did offer me the job, and it paid well. I knew God was in this opportunity, so I did not hesitate to accept the offer. I would be starting in two weeks. I couldn't wait to tell Sheila the good news!

Sheila took off from work the next day so we could search for an apartment. It turned out that Vanessa, another of our close college friends, was also living in Dallas. Sheila and Vanessa, whom we affectionately called "Bug," had been in contact because Bug was also looking for a new place to stay. We decided to look for a place large enough for the three of us to live together. That same day, we found a three-bedroom apartment in Valley Ranch that was just four miles from my new job and less than five miles from where my new roommates were already working. It was perfect! By that weekend, we had moved in and decorated our beautiful new home.

I came to town on Sunday, got a job on Monday, and found a place to live on Tuesday. It couldn't have been more obvious to me that God's hand was on the move to Dallas. All that remained was for me to find a good church home. Although Sheila believed in God, she had not committed her life to him at the time. She was very respectful of my faith and open to Bible study. Knowing how important it was to me, she had compiled a list of churches for me to check out. On her list was Highland Oaks Church of Christ. It was a forty-mile drive from Valley Ranch, but it turned out to be well worth the trek. There we were on a Wednesday night, sitting together at this church far from our home, but it somehow felt like home. I could tell that Sheila enjoyed the service too, and this was just one more confirmation to me that this was where we should attend.

My first two weeks in Dallas flew by. I had found a job, an apartment, roommates, and a church home without the tiniest struggle. Everything in my life was falling into place, and I constantly offered praise and thanksgiving to God for his goodness. I kept the lines of communication open back home with friends and family and gave them cheerful updates on my new life in Dallas.

My new job was in health care administration, which was very different from accounting, but I enjoyed it immensely. I found great favor with my coworkers and was easily forming friendships. Janet, a single mother with two children, decided to take me under her wing. She went the extra mile to train me, showing me love, patience, and kindness as I learned to do my job. In just three short months, I was promoted from supervisor to manager. I was overjoyed.

I became more and more involved at Highland Oaks and was active in church events and ministry. Sheila and Bug, along with another friend, started attending with me on a regular basis. It was a long drive, but we visited together during the commute and enjoyed the services immensely. Within two months, Sheila gave her life to Jesus Christ. The day she was baptized was one of the happiest days of my life. We had been best friends for seven years, and I loved her like family.

We rejoiced together in sweet celebration of this new chapter in her life.

We continued at Highland Oaks Church of Christ, and while I knew it was an important time in Sheila's spiritual development, I began to pray that God would guide us to a church closer to home where we could be more involved.

One day, to our surprise, a couple knocked on our door. We rarely had guests, and if we did, they were expected, so the knock startled us. We lived on the third floor, so if someone had put in enough energy to climb all those stairs, we knew it must be important. We opened the door to meet Kevin and Sandra Moses. They smiled warmly and invited us to attend a Church of Christ, which was just starting up in Coppell in a nearby office building. The congregation was small but filled with sincere people who loved God. There weren't many ministers there, and few activities, but we were eager to assist in building this new ministry. For a season, we attended both Highland Oaks Church of Christ and the Coppell Church of Christ, but finally decided to put all our energies into the new church. Once again, a new beginning called for a necessary ending.

PART 3

Love and Warning Signs

CHAPTER 11

Finding Love

Falling in love consists merely of
uncorking the imagination and
bottling the common sense.

Helen Rowland

My life settled into a nice routine. I was happy. I was content. I was filled with God's joy, growing in his Word, enjoying my roommates, thriving at my job, and excited to wake up every morning to greet a new day.

Enter a mysterious stranger.

It was December 1986, and I had been living in Dallas for about four months. I was on my way out of town for the weekend and needed to make a quick stop at my insurance agent's office and the bank, both of which were conveniently located in the same building. I went first to see my agent and from there to the bank. At the bank, I noticed a man staring at me, and it wasn't the first time. In fact, it seemed like nearly every time I visited the bank or the agent, he was there, staring at me. I immediately left the line at the bank, feeling nervous and uncomfortable. I went back to my insurance agent's office to wait, hoping the man would leave so I could go back and conduct my bank business in peace. The stranger's gaze was too much for me. Whatever advances he planned on making, I wasn't interested.

Once inside the insurance office, the agent wondered what was wrong and asked if I was okay. When I explained the situation, the agent asked me if I knew who this man was. I acknowledged that I had, in fact, seen him a few times on television and knew who he was, but I wasn't interested.

"You know he's a professional athlete, right?" the agent asked.

"Not interested," I said and gave him a smile. "I just want to finish my business and hit the road for Louisiana. Tomorrow is my birthday, and I feel like going home!"

"Wow, happy birthday!" he said, and then added, "To tell you the truth, this guy has been asking around about you. He really wants to meet you."

Here I had been thinking this guy kept showing up by chance, and now it was obvious it had been intentional. It unnerved me.

"Forget it," I said, sweeping out of the insurance office. "I'll stop by the bank some other time." I headed for my car, never looking back. But when I got to the parking lot, there he was, draped across my car and smiling from ear to ear.

"Hi," he said casually, "my name is Nathaniel, but most people just call me Nate. Would you join me for dinner?"

"No, thank you," I said forcefully. "I don't care who you are. I'm in a hurry, and I need to get down the road."

"Where you going in such a hurry?" he replied, still smiling.

I let out an irritated sigh. "I'm on my way to visit my family in Louisiana if you must know," I answered.

"Well, can I have your phone number at least? I'd like to call you sometime."

I squared my shoulders and faced him. Politely, yet sternly I replied, "I don't give my number to strangers."

"Well, I'm not exactly a stranger, now, am I?" Undaunted, he flashed another smile attempting to disarm me.

"I'll tell you what," he said cheerfully. "How 'bout I give you my number and you can give me a call when you have a little more time? Would that be alright?" He looked hopeful.

I said nothing. I stared at the ground and wondered how to escape this uncomfortable situation. This big man was blocking me from entering my car.

"Now me — I'm from Orlando, Florida," he said, taking a

different approach. "That's quite a drive from Dallas, let me tell you. How long of a drive is it for you to get to New Orleans?"

My curt responses never disheartened him. He easily moved from one topic to the next, as if our conversation was a natural exchange between two longtime friends. He seemed totally unaffected by how chilly and closed I was to his advances.

"What's the weather like in New Orleans?" he asked, trying yet another approach.

"Okay," I said, "if I take your number and call you, I can answer all your questions then." I had no intention of calling him, but I thought taking his number might get him to finally let me leave.

He looked at me intently, then his features softened once more into a relaxed gaze. "Please, just one more question," he said. "If you answer it, I promise not to take up any more of your time."

I stared at him in disbelief. How could he still want to talk to me after I'd so clearly rejected him?

"Why won't you talk to me after I've made so many attempts?" he asked.

"Look," I said in exasperation, "I know who you are. I know you play football for the Dallas Cowboys. I'm just not interested in getting to know you. Why is that such a big deal?" Not even this put him off. He held me captive there for at least another thirty minutes talking about anything and everything.

At last I interrupted him. "Listen, if I don't leave now I'll be late for my birthday celebration back home. Please let me go."

"Is it really your birthday?" he said with new excitement.

"Tomorrow. Saturday. The twentieth," I said matter-of-factly.

He started laughing uncontrollably. "This is definitely meant to happen on this day," he said. "I can't believe it. I just can't believe it!"

"What are you talking about?" I said, annoyed, but now a bit intrigued.

"Tomorrow is my birthday too!" he said.

I must have looked very skeptical because he immediately pulled out his wallet to show me his driver's license as proof. His birthday was, in fact, the very next day—the same day, the same year as mine.

This inspired yet another thirty minutes of conversation. I looked him over carefully and handed back his phone number. He looked surprised.

"If you really want to contact me, call this," I said, writing my number on a slip of paper and handing it to him.

"I will do that!" he said, grinning broadly. I got in my car, giving him a smile and a wave as I drove off, heading home for the weekend.

The truth was that there would be no birthday celebration for me at home. Since my mother had become a Jehovah's Witness, there were no more birthday celebrations. Still, I wanted to be near my family on my birthday. On the trip home, I kept replaying the odd exchange between Nate and myself but then dismissed it. *That's probably the last time I'll ever see him*, I thought.

When I returned to Dallas late Sunday night and checked my answering machine, there were several messages from Nate. He was just as persistent with his phone calls as he had been with our face-to-face conversation. We soon became faithful telephone friends and sometimes spent hours talking to each other. After several weeks of talking only on the phone, Nate persisted in asking me out for a date. At first I refused, but I was eventually softened by his many attempts. I finally told him I'd be happy to go on a date with him, as long as it was on my terms.

By this time, I was playing recreational volleyball. I decided my volleyball tournament that Saturday would be our first official "date." After the game he said he'd enjoyed watching me play, but he didn't understand why this had to be our first date. I told him I wanted him to see me when I was hot and sweaty—without any makeup. Then, if he still wanted to take me out on a date, I would go. He laughed that charming laugh, and I melted. I really did like him. We left the game and ate burgers and talked with each other for a long time. I spent our whole first date wearing my sweaty clothes from the game. From that point on, we began spending a lot of time together.

When I met Nate, he was a free agent playing left guard for the Dallas Cowboys. This was during the time that William "The Refrigerator" Perry achieved fame playing for the Chicago Bears. Nate was even larger than Perry, and so he was nick-named "The Kitchen." Nate explained that because he was a free agent, he would have to try out with the Cowboys each season, and not one season was guaranteed to the next. He also told me he had left his previous team, the Washington Redskins, by his own volition, when in reality he'd been cut from the team. Immediately following his dismissal, he was in a car accident, which had been plastered across the media headlines as an alleged suicide attempt.

Many of our conversations revolved around our difficult life experiences and the type of people we had become as a result. I learned that Nate's birth mother was an alcoholic and that he had been raised by his father. The woman Nate called Mom was his father's second wife. Nate also told me about playing football for Florida A&M, but he acknowledged that his time in college was not something he was proud of. During this current season in his life, he said he wanted to put his old life behind him. I thought I had experienced a lot of struggles during my childhood, but I soon realized that Nate was no stranger to trials and tribulations. We were both carrying baggage.

When I listened to him talk about his past, the setbacks, and the mistakes, I felt an enormous amount of compassion for him and had a desire to share Christ with him. The vulnerability he demonstrated in sharing the painful episodes from his life made my heart warm up toward him even more.

Still, I had some reservations. Nate was not a Christian man—and he didn't pretend to be. In fact, he had this twisted belief that before you could come to God you had to first be a good person. Since he didn't think he was a good enough person, somehow he wasn't qualified to be a Christian. I honestly thought I could change his point of view.

"You can't be a good person without Christ," I reasoned. "None of us can. You don't have to be a good person to know him in the first place. You can't truly be a good person *until* you know him."

I brought up the possibility once again of doing Bible study together. I knew I didn't have all of the answers, but I believed I could help him along the way. I was sure that what had worked for me would work for him too. I wanted so desperately for him to understand what I understood about the love of God and how fulfilling and peaceful his life could be. For the longest time, I viewed my relationship with Nate simply as an opportunity to share Christ with him. I had convinced myself that God put Nate in my path just so I could minister to him.

As time went on, however, I could no longer fool myself. I realized how much I loved Nate—not just because I wanted to share Christ with him, but because I was in love with him. I believed that in time he would come to know the Lord, and all of his struggles and problems would be in God's hands. I knew he wasn't perfect and it was going to take time for him to change. He asked me to be patient. He confessed he had not been the best person in the past and that he knew he probably wouldn't be the best person in the future. But he promised to do whatever it took to refrain from living like his old self. He wanted a new life, to be a better person. He wanted us to be together and grow together in love. I believed he was open to Christ, and there was evidence he was softening. I trusted that he wanted to become a Christian.

Although our relationship was moving in a positive direction, Nate's professional life was plagued by negativity. He had experienced several difficulties during the mini-football camp with the Cowboys in the spring. He was extremely overweight, and his poor showing at the mini-camp made headlines: "Nate Newton, Battle of the Bulge." "The Fat Guy." "He's too fat, he can't move." It seemed like every time we picked up a newspaper or turned on the television, there were quotes and comments about him — all unfavorable.

The more Nate became aware of the criticism, the harder it was for him to accomplish his goals. When we were together, he often asked me to pray for him out loud so he could hear me. He wanted to know how I was praying for him and what I was saying to God. I prayed that Nate would see God personally and not just through me. I wanted him to accept God into his heart and see that nothing was impossible with God.

We spent the entire spring season working out together. I was in great shape and enjoyed the discipline of exercising with Nate. We exercised our bodies and trained our minds. By the time June came around and training camp began, Nate had reached his conditioning goals. In fact, he not only met the weight requirements; he was also in the best shape ever. I was so happy when he gave credit to God for what God had done for him. Nate started to believe in himself and to believe in the power of prayer—at least in the power of my prayers on his behalf. Nate made the team that year and landed a starting position as an offensive guard for the Dallas Cowboys.

He told me he now understood that being cut from the Redskins was part of God's plan for him to play with the Dallas Cowboys—his dream team. Being on that team was something he and his best friend, Tony Hayes (T. Hayes), had always dreamed about. Now it was a reality. He was a free agent—signing a contract with incentives as a starter. We celebrated his accomplishments, and I began to see Nate as a man with a lot of courage, hope, and faith. I admired him. He never gave up, and he worked hard to press on. I was proud of him. I was happy for him. I was in love with him.

CHAPTER 12

Nate Newton's Girl

Love is an endless act of forgiveness.

Peter Ustinov

I loved going to church. It was as natural to me as shopping for groceries or going to school. Every week I looked forward to singing and worshiping the Lord, being fortified with the Word through sermons, and visiting with people who loved God.

Now Nate was in the picture. The Cowboys played on Sundays, and Nate wanted me to attend every home game. I loved watching him play, and it felt good knowing Nate Newton cared that I was there. I sat in the stands beaming with pride. I was Nate Newton's girl!

At first I tried to juggle things, but there wasn't a way to be actively involved in church on Sundays and still go to the games. Slowly, my involvement in church decreased. I justified it because I was still diligent with prayer and Bible study on my own. Plus, I was Nate's personal witness, and I desperately wanted Nate to know the Lord.

⌒⌒

It was the fall of 1987, and the Cowboys were not playing well that season. It was a difficult time for the whole team. I saw my role as an encourager. Nate often asked me to pray for him and for the Cowboys, and he seemed very sincere in his requests. He believed my prayers made a difference and called me a woman of God.

With each passing week, I fell deeper and deeper in love with this man—it was intoxicating. He was meeting deep emotional needs for me, and I was growing to trust him more and more. I found it increasingly difficult to balance my love for Nate and my love for God. I always wanted God to be first, but Nate kept slipping into that position, and I was in a constant state of unrest.

It bothered me that Nate had not yet accepted Christ as his Savior, even though he clearly believed that Jesus was God's son. I couldn't grasp why he wouldn't give his life to Jesus since he obviously believed in God and in the power of prayer. I often asked Nate to come to church with me, but he never would. He was completely fine with me going to church, reading the Bible, praying, and even talking to him about God — in fact, he was more than fine, he was supportive. He just wasn't interested in a relationship with God for himself. As long as he had me, and I was close to God — that was close enough for him.

When the team's performance improved, the media attention increased, and this time it was positive. Everybody loved Nate Newton — they just couldn't get enough of his charismatic personality. But the more positive attention he received, the less inclined he was to talk about God. Now that Nate was on top, he didn't seem to need my prayers. God was reserved for the low times. I decided I needed to be patient with him and not nag him about it. I was sure that if I spent time with him and my life was full of God's love, eventually Nate would come to the decision to accept Christ on his own. Nate was such a great guy, and he made me feel special. How could it not work out? I just needed to give him some time.

It was wonderful to be fascinating to someone. People had always sought me out to share their problems, ask for my advice, or have me pray for them, but no one had ever expressed the kind of interest in me that Nate did. He was interested in my job and encouraged me to talk about my day, my friends—anything that was on my mind. Whenever I got quiet, he'd ask questions to draw me out. He complimented me and made me feel beautiful. Nate's interest was more than flattering; it was fulfilling. I felt valued and precious to him, and I liked the feeling.

There were so many things I loved about Nate. He was generous with his time and his personality. No one could brighten a room or lift a mood like Nate could. Sometimes he would take me out with my roommates and his best friend Tony Hayes, whom we called T. Hayes. We'd drive somewhere, have dinner, and laugh the night away. If Nate was there, it was a party!

Nate had wonderful manners. He was a gentleman—respectful of authority, respectful toward me. He was a leader and an influencer. People were naturally drawn to him, and this quality was very attractive to me. I imagined what a powerful influence he could be if only he finally yielded his life to Christ.

Nate made me feel safe, and this was no small thing. For the first time in my life, I felt like I had a protector. I didn't feel like it was up to me to handle everything. I knew he would never let anyone harm me. Even on days when I felt ugly, Nate would look me in the eyes and tell me I was beautiful, inside and out. He put me on a pedestal, and it was fun being there.

Family was important to Nate. He treated my family well and was especially kind to my mother. This touched me deeply. I could imagine raising a family with him—a modest house somewhere near Dallas with a few children running around on the lawn, going to Cowboys games together, and having people over for the holidays. It was a beautiful picture in my mind, far from the dysfunction I had grown up with. It was a dream I wanted very much to make a reality.

Nate listened attentively when I talked about my relationship with God. He somehow knew my connection to God was what made me special. He was interested in Christianity and asked questions about it too, but he didn't feel he was good enough to become a Christian. He knew that if he gave his life to Christ, he'd have to give up a lot of things he enjoyed doing, and he just wasn't ready for that. I appreciated his honesty. In fact, I took it as a good sign that he was willing to listen to me and not pretend. I never stopped communicating or spending time with him because of his reluctance. I didn't want to seem judgmental, and I knew that if I pulled away, it would hurt Nate. He was so open and accepting of me, my beliefs, and everything that was important in my life, and I wanted to return this level of openness and respect to him.

I had hoped I was being a positive influence on Nate, but I was finding that the more time we spent together, the more his behavior slipped. His language went from being always respectful to an occasional slip of the tongue to regular use of profanity. He drank beer too much and too often. He sometimes said mean things. I had never experienced him that way before, and I didn't like it. Warning signs were flashing red in my mind and spirit, but somehow I always managed to shrug away his troublesome behavior: *No one changes overnight, after all; it takes time.* Again, I decided to be patient with him in the hope that if I could continue being a good influence, it would make a difference. I encouraged him to be better, to be his best. When he behaved badly, I told myself he was wrestling with his old nature, that it had a firm grip on him but would release him when he committed his life to Christ.

Over time, my patience with his behavior slipped into compromising my own standards. Little by little, Nate was changing, but not in the ways I'd hoped. Still, I continued to excuse his behavior by telling myself that a change for the better was coming soon.

As time went on, however, the open, free-flowing com-munication we'd once had began to dwindle. I could tell that something was bothering Nate, but since he wouldn't open up to me about what it was, I couldn't seem to help him through it. His behavior grew more reckless, and he was agitated and angry more often. Instead of sharing his most personal thoughts with me and taking me into his confidence, he now seemed guarded. I tried to write it off to the stress of so much publicity and the growing pressure to perform well at every game. But there was no denying that Nate was changing—and not for the better. The change was apparent to everyone, and it troubled me. But every time a black cloud hovered over our relationship, Nate found a way to make the sun come out again. I was determined to be as supportive as I knew how to be, and Nate seemed calmer when I was around, so 1 took this as a good sign. Things would be okay.

CHAPTER 13

Love Is a Wonderful Thing

When a heart finds another, what's
a cloud more or less in the sky.

Peter Wolf, Ina Wolf, and Martin Page

Nate and I were better than ever. We were meeting each other's friends and getting to know each other's families. I believed he was the one I would spend the rest of my life with. More and more, I could look at the future and imagine growing old with Nate Newton at my side.

Still, I was plagued by a nagging unrest about where he was in his relationship with God. I knew he believed in God, but when the conversation turned to salvation, Nate would always say he wasn't good enough yet. He hated hypocrites and vowed never to be one. He didn't want to pretend he was a Christian, and since he was straddling the fence with one foot securely in the world and the other uncomfortably entertaining the possibility of being a Christian, he wasn't ready to accept Christ.

I loved God deeply and wanted to please him in everything I did, but there was a tug-of-war in my heart. When I was alone with God, I was totally filled with peace and secure in his love for me. When I was alone with Nate, God receded to the background. My connection to Nate increased my physical attraction, and all I could think about was sexual intimacy with him.

When I was a young girl, I made a conscious decision to wait for sex until I fell in love and married. My mom had warned me about the dangers of being unequally yoked, and I knew better than to marry a man who was not a Christian. Nate clearly felt differently than I did, but he respected my position. He thought it was okay, even good, for dating couples to engage in sex. I believed it was wrong. I had remained pure. Now here I was, still a virgin and deeply in love, but beginning to feel guilty for making my future husband wait when I was the one who wasn't ready yet to be married. My resolve wavered and then gave way.

I made a decision to go on birth control pills. I decided that if I was going to betray my morals, the last thing I wanted was to bring a baby into the equation. My doctor was a wise, kind, Christian man. He counseled me to wait, even as he reluctantly wrote out a prescription. Even there in the doctor's office, I had second thoughts about it. Going on the pill was deciding to have sex outside of marriage. I knew I was making a conscious decision to sin.

Nate and I planned it. It was anything but a spontaneous burst of passion. It wasn't a magical night in which we lost control and were swept up in the heat of the moment. In truth, "the moment" had been building for months. Looking back, it's hard for me to reconcile these two things: I wasn't ready to commit to Nate in marriage because he had not yet made a commitment to Christ; yet somehow I did feel ready to commit to the acts of marriage with Nate. It no longer seemed important to wait until the wedding bells had rung. I was an adult after all. I was in love. We were in love. Wasn't that what really mattered?

Nate and I were playing house. It was like a trial run to see if marriage would work out. I never wanted to be in a situation like my mother, financially dependent on a man and unable to escape if things went wrong. As much as I loved Nate, I wasn't ready to walk down the aisle and commit my life to him forever. I needed some measure of control. I didn't want to be married. Things were good just like they were for now. Nate seemed content to be with me on these terms, and in my mind, this left me free to walk away if I needed to.

I often traveled to be with Nate for away games, and sometimes his family would join us. One weekend, they came to Dallas for a home game, arriving on a chartered bus from Florida. I went to the hotel with Nate to greet his family. I had met several people from his family at previous games, so I was excited to see them again and interested to see who else came along that I had not yet met.

To my great surprise, a long-lost girlfriend had come to town to see Nate. I was shocked. Nate's family was clearly embarrassed by the situation. They apologized profusely. They knew Nate and I were close. They knew how important I was to Nate. Why this woman had chosen to come along, knowing I would be there, is a mystery I have never understood. Of course, this all happened the day before the game — after the Cowboys had sequestered all their players in a hotel to keep them focused on the task at hand. They didn't want their star athletes distracted by anything that might hinder their performance in the game. So Nate was not around to see me in my misery or to answer my questions. He wasn't there to face the music, own up to his deceit, and explain his lies.

I felt so betrayed. I thought I was special to him. I had been totally faithful to him. He was the only man I had ever given myself to, and the thought of him being with someone else felt like a kick in the stomach. I felt ill.

Nate's family was sensitive to my struggle. I could tell they were sincere in their concern, so I dug down deep, found every ounce of kindness I could muster, and pressed through the game rituals with a pasted smile on my face to support Nate. I don't remember much about the game because I was too busy working through all the things I wanted to ask Nate on the way home. The more I thought about it, the more I realized this was an opportunity to make a clean break and get out.

I recognized how much I had lost my focus—on God, my career, and even family goals. I had become totally absorbed in Nate's world, Nate's future, and Nate's needs, and I had lost myself in the process.

After the game, Nate's family said good-bye and got back on the bus headed for Florida. It was time for Nate and me to have a heart-to-heart talk. I decided I didn't want to have anything to do with him anymore. I had been with him for almost two years, and he never mentioned he had a girlfriend during the same time he was dating me. I was hurt and angry. I didn't want to talk about it—no explanations; I just wanted to make a break from Nate and move on. I should have done it long before, and this was the jolt I needed to wake up from my fairy tale and enter the land of reality.

Instead of confronting Nate and asking him to explain his deception, I chose to distance myself from him. I refused to accept his phone calls. I wouldn't answer my door. I was devastated by his betrayal.

I decided that this might be a good time to move back home to Louisiana. Because I still had three months on my lease, I gave three months' notice at my job, packed all my things and placed them in storage. I would use only the bare essentials in my apartment until my lease expired and I was free to move home. I hadn't made any plans about where I would go in Louisiana, where I would live, or where I would work, but I was focused on this new course of action and determined that everything would work out just as it should.

I stopped taking the pill. I regretted I had ever started taking it. I regretted surrendering my virginity. I made the determination that I was through with Nate Newton—for good!

Nate kept dropping by my office and coming to my apartment trying to talk to me. He was doing everything he possibly could to stop me from leaving. I felt like he was stalking me; every time I turned around, there he was! After four solid weeks of this, I relented and let him in one night. I wanted him to see I was serious. I thought if he saw my apartment bare and knew I was resolute in my decision to move away from him and move on with my life, it might make him realize our relationship was truly over.

Nate asked me to just listen to what he had to say. He was so earnest that I didn't have the power to refuse. He told me he had not been spending time with the young woman and had not seen her for a very long time. They had bought a house together and he was helping her out financially. He told me they were no longer in a relationship and that he was as surprised as anyone that she showed up at the game. He was sorry I was hurt—that he had hurt me. He was desperate for me to believe him and forgive him.

For days, he kept coming to my apartment and stopping by my office, and each time he always seemed to have just the right things to say. To put me at even greater ease, he communicated with the woman on the telephone in my presence, so I could hear what he said and be assured there was no relationship between them. My resolve wavered.

Nate produced receipts to show me he had given this woman a lump sum of money to help her out. He assured me over and over again that it was me he wanted to spend his life with. He was so sincere and took such extreme measures to prove himself that I couldn't help but believe him. *Maybe I wasn't being fair to Nate*, I thought.

I took my things out of storage and weighed my options. What should I do? Before this incident with the woman, our relationship had its ups and downs, but there had been nothing like this—nothing that made me lose trust in him or feel betrayed. I still loved Nate, and part of me wanted to forgive him and move on. *Was my love strong enough to overcome the pain? Could I trust Nate? Should I stay in Dallas and give our relationship another chance, or should I move home to Louisiana and forget all about Nate Newton?*

I decided to stay. I withdrew my resignation from my job, and they were thrilled I was staying. Nate and I started seeing each other, and things were good again. I forgave Nate, and he went out of his way to make sure he didn't hide things from me. He knew I was serious enough to leave my job and move away from him, and this had a profound impact on Nate. He didn't want to jeopardize what we had and grew more determined for us to be a lifelong partnership.

Nate even agreed with me that God was the only way our relationship would work. Though he wasn't ready to go to church, he consented to do a Bible study with me and another couple from my church. I was still shaken from the incident with the girl from Florida, but I saw it as an opportunity for us to strengthen our bond and establish trust, and for Nate to finally commit his life to the Lord. I knew that total forgiveness was required from me, and I gave it.

Still, at times I caught myself looking in the mirror and wondered who it was that was staring back at me. Once confident and bold, I had become unsure of myself. I missed my close relationship with God. I still knew him and trusted him, but I was no longer deeply intimate with him. The sense of loss was overwhelming. I felt God calling me to return to him.

Nate invited me to take a trip with him to Atlanta. Road trips with Nate were the best. And maybe that was just what we needed right then. It was a lovely drive, and we were never in a hurry. We took our time to stop and see anything that captured our interest. We talked comfortably about everything and were totally at ease with one another. We met up with friends of his and shared the most beautiful four-day weekend together.

Our first night together on the road, I reminded Nate that I had only been back on the pill for one week. He brushed it off, reassuring me that nothing would happen, that I should trust him. We were both aware of the risks, but neither one of us thought for one moment that I would conceive. The pill was our magic shield against responsibility.

From then on, we were sexually intimate on a regular basis, so I don't know exactly when it happened. But early in February, my family came into town, and I was feeling a little sick. When I complained of nausea, my mother looked me right in the eyes and said, "Dorothy, you're not pregnant, are you?"

"Mama! No!" I exclaimed. "How can you say that?" Being pregnant never entered my mind. I felt safe on the pill.

It wasn't until a full two months later that I realized the truth. I was stunned. *How could this have happened?* We never used any extra protection because I was taking birth control pills, and the "98 percent effective" promise sounded like pretty good odds. I felt protected from the risk, so I was willing to take it.

In those moments of passion and intimacy, God was the last thing on my mind. And my fears of being unequally yoked to Nate in marriage somehow didn't translate into a fear of creating a soul tie with this man through our sexual relationship or the possibility of creating a baby in the process. But I had made my choice, and I knew what I was doing. It was a decision that changed my life forever.

CHAPTER 14

Shattered Dreams

"For I know the plans I have for you,"
declares the LORD, "plans to prosper you
and not to harm you, plans to give
you hope and a future."

Jeremiah 29:11 NIV

God's best for my life was all I had ever wanted. No longer did that seem possible. I stared down at the pregnancy test in disbelief. I read the instructions once more, hoping that maybe I had done something wrong to make the test inaccurate. But there was no denying it: I was pregnant.

I looked in the mirror and felt sick. The woman who stared back at me was a stranger. She looked lost and confused and totally without hope. The sadness in her eyes was unbearable. I turned away and crumpled in a heap on the floor. I had never felt so alone. What a mess! What was I going to do? What would my family say? *Oh, Mama!*

I grabbed a towel and hugged it to my chest, squeezing it until my knuckles hurt and my hands were shaking. My mind went to all the people I had studied the Bible with in college. I thought about everyone I had witnessed to and how many of them had come to know the Lord. I could see their faces. I felt as if I had let every one of them down. I was a fraud. *How could I have been so stupid?* Those thoughts overwhelmed me with grief and sorrow. Then I tried to imagine what God must think of me and how I had turned my back on him. Sobs shook my body. I don't know how long I lay there crying, but I cried until there were no tears left. I was disgusted with myself. *Oh, what had I done?*

I grew cold lying there on the floor. Shame and fear gave way to pity, and depression settled over me like a dark, ominous cloud. Then my thoughts wandered to Nate. *What would he think? How would he react?* I didn't really blame him; I was too filled with blaming myself. *How would I tell him? What would he say?*

I avoided him for days, not sure how to break the news. I was miserable. Doubt, fear, frustration, anger — my emotions were boiling just beneath the surface, and I found it hard to concentrate on anything.

I went to see my doctor, and he confirmed that I was, in fact, pregnant. He seemed sad for me and asked about the father. I told him who it was. In a very kind gesture, he invited me to have dinner with him and his wife in their home. I was so desperate and alone that I accepted. They prayed for me and were supportive and encouraging without one hint of judgment. I was overwhelmed by their kindness.

Later, I called Sheila, my college roommate and best friend, and asked to meet her. Even though we were both wrapped up in our separate lives, our bond was still close, and I knew I needed to tell her the news in person.

"I'm pregnant," I blurted out, not sure how else to begin. I knew Sheila wouldn't judge me. She hugged me tightly and held me with such kindness. Her voice was tender. "Dot, I saw you drifting away. You were so in love that I didn't want to interfere."

Tears rolled down my cheeks, I felt so ashamed. I was grateful for her friendship at this moment. Sharing my burden with her was such a relief. "What should I do?" I asked, not really expecting an answer.

"Don't worry," she smiled, "we're going to get through this."

After talking to Sheila, I knew I needed to call Bug, the mother hen in our little trio. At first she fussed at me. "I could see this coming. You haven't been the same person since Nate. I tried to tell you" — and on and on she went. Then her voice softened, and her affection for me came shining through. "Everything is gonna be alright. Everything is gonna work out just fine. You'll see." We talked for quite some time, and I felt less alone. Now I just needed to tell Nate.

I gathered my courage. It was clear to me that the people who loved me might be disappointed in me, but they would still love me. I was sure it would be the same with Nate.

Nate and I had dinner plans to visit with our friends Lynn and Kelvin (K-Mart) Martin that Friday night, so I decided to tell Nate on Thursday. He came by the apartment as usual, and since I had been avoiding him for a few days, things were a little tense. We were usually together every day, so this break in the routine had left him wary.

"What is wrong with you?" he asked.

"Nathaniel," I looked at him, hoping he would just guess the trouble so I wouldn't have to actually say the words.

He looked at me intently, sensing I was about to tell him something important. I could see the muscles in his neck tighten, and his face was a mixture of concern and frustration.

"Nathaniel, I'm pregnant."

"You're what?" he said. "You knew I didn't want any kids!" he shouted.

I stared at him in shock.

"You knew what we were doing, Nathaniel Newton!" I answered, suddenly angry. "It wasn't like I was trying to trap you or anything. Having a baby wasn't part of my plan either."

We argued for some time, angry words spilling out from both of us until Nate walked out cursing and slammed the door behind him.

I hadn't been prepared for such an outburst of rage. I didn't expect him to be overjoyed, but I never dreamed he would be so angry—and so angry with me.

An hour passed. I sat alone, numb. My mind couldn't seem to make two thoughts line up in a row. Random bits of information flooded my mind, but none of it made any sense. Then there was a knock at the door, and Nate had returned. He was still mad.

"Why are you so upset?" I asked.

"What about me?" was his response. "How do you think I feel?"

I just stared back at him, not sure how to answer. He walked across the room, sat down, sighed deeply, and then told me he already had two children and didn't want any more.

I was stunned. I don't know how long I sat there trying to take in this new information. *Did I really even know this man at all?*

"Why didn't you ever tell me?" I finally managed to ask.

"What does it matter to you?" he said.

I couldn't believe that Nate had children out there somewhere. *Who were they? Where did they live? Did he see them? Who was their mother? How old? Boys? Girls?* I couldn't stop the questions, but I didn't voice a single one of them to Nate. I didn't dare.

I had taken most of the next day off from work, knowing I was going to tell Nate that night and somehow sensing it might not go well. This only increased his anger toward me.

"Why didn't you save the vacation day so we could take a trip?" he asked. Nate loved nothing more than road trips, and during the off-season he had more free time available than I did, so I had been using my vacation days for trips with Nate.

"I thought this was important," I answered, hurt that he was being so selfish.

Nate responded with a barrage of insults and accusations, blaming me for the pregnancy. I answered with indignation, blaming him for his lies. The argument continued, escalating until Nate left again, hurling profanities as he slammed the door on his way out.

The next morning I went into the office to go to a meeting. Nate showed up as I sat at my desk after the meeting had ended.

"I thought you took the day off?" he said, accusation thick in his voice.

"I just came in for a one-hour meeting," I answered. "I'm getting ready to go now." Nate nodded, and we walked out in silence. He had his arm lightly on my elbow and directed me toward his truck.

"Get in," he said while calmly opening the passenger door for me. I slid into my familiar place, closing my eyes and wishing I could make this nightmare end.

Nate walked around to the driver's side, opened the door, and climbed inside. He sat there quietly for a few moments, then reached over and took my hand. "We'll work it out," he said, his voice soft and low.

I felt my muscles relax, and I let out a long sigh. This was the Nate I knew. I leaned over and melted into his embrace. It felt good to be held by him. I didn't want to do this alone.

We sat in the parking lot for a while, and Nate told me he still wanted to go to the Martins together that night. He wanted to tell them about the baby. This was encouraging to me. Maybe everything really would work out okay. Maybe Nate would be just fine about it after all.

We went to dinner as planned. Lynn and K-Mart were good friends, and being with them felt natural. Nate told them the news, and I was surprised at how upbeat and nonchalant he sounded. Surprise, surprise! Lynn and K-Mart had news for us—they were expecting too! Suddenly it was a party! We learned that our due dates were very close together. Lynn and I had lots to talk about, and Nate seemed to be very excited about the prospect of having a baby. I was never so relieved!

The next day, I decided it was time to call my family. There was no point in putting it off any longer. I called my mom first. "I knew you were pregnant, Dorothy," she said. "I could tell the moment I saw you. I've been wondering when you were going to call."

It felt good to talk to Mom. She was so understanding, and I knew she would be there for me and love me, no matter what. "Dorothy," she said, "you be smart about this. Don't settle. No matter what happens, don't you get rid of that baby. If Nate doesn't want it, we'll take it. Don't you even think about getting an abortion. That isn't a solution."

Her words struck me. I wasn't even aware I had considered the possibility of aborting, but her strong warning suddenly shook me. In the back of my mind, I had played with the idea that abortion might be a way out. Of course it wasn't!

There was no way I was going to deal with one sin by committing another. Just like that, my mind was resolved. I would not abort. I would not give up my baby. It was mine. Nate or no Nate, this baby was in my life for good. Something broke inside me, and I was filled with overwhelming love for the life that was growing inside me.

When I began telling friends about the baby, I was overwhelmed with love and support. I didn't feel judged. I didn't feel an outcast. Instead, I felt genuine kindness, and my heart was filled with hope.

I began reading about pregnancy and babies, learning everything I could. I carefully calculated my savings and took a long look at my financial situation to make sure I was prepared. It had been three weeks since I first told Nate the news, and the excitement he demonstrated with the Martins had steadily waned. This bothered me, but I assumed he was just working through things in his mind.

He came by my apartment one night and was unusually quiet. "I know this isn't your fault," he began. "This is *our* problem."

I looked at him cautiously, wondering where he was going with this.

"It's my responsibility. I want to take care of this. I've thought about it a lot since you first told me you were pregnant." He paused. I held my breath.

"I think you should get an abortion," he said flatly. "I'll pay for it. I'll take care of everything. I just don't think having a baby is the best thing for us right now."

Nate slowly exhaled. I could tell he had made up his mind. All I had to do was say yes, and the problem would be solved. I sat in silence, wrestling with my emotions. I thought I had settled this already.

Deep down inside, I was still struggling with how I had failed God. I was struggling with shame and guilt. I was angry with myself for compromising. I was angry that the birth control pills hadn't worked. I was angry that Nate wasn't treating me the same anymore. He had grown cold—there was a meanness in him toward me that I had never seen before, and it scared me. I didn't really want to have Nate's baby. I wasn't even sure I wanted to have Nate anymore. I wavered.

"I'll think about it," I said.

Nate looked at me and started to say something, but the look on my face must have stopped him. "Fine," he said. "Let me know when you make the appointment and I'll take care of it."

I got some literature and went to a clinic to ask about an abortion. I even made an appointment, but I couldn't go in. I sat outside in the parking lot with the words of the prophet

Jeremiah running through my head, "Before I formed you in the womb I knew you" (Jeremiah 1:5 NKJV). God already knew this baby. This baby was already his child. I just could *not* make another bad choice. No. I was not going to give this baby up just to make my life less complicated. The child had done nothing to deserve being erased. The child was innocent. The child had no choice, even if I did. Abortion was not the answer. I drove away from the clinic and never gave abortion another thought.

When Nate came by later that evening, I told him I was going to keep the baby. He was very angry. He argued and cursed. He insulted me and made me feel selfish, but he could not persuade me. I didn't care how angry he was. I didn't care if he left me forever. My mind was made up. I told him he didn't need to worry about anything. I had no expectations from him. The decision to keep the baby was mine. I would take care of the baby. I would raise the baby. I would pay for the baby. I wanted nothing from Nate Newton. He didn't need to worry about anything. He was free to go.

CHAPTER 15

Ultimatum

The one who loves the least,
controls the relationship.

Robert Anthony

Nate was not happy with my decision to keep the baby. He gave me an ultimatum: "Have an abortion, or we're finished."

I thought Nate truly loved me. He was the one who wanted to get married and live happily ever after. How could he leave me over a baby—his own baby? It didn't make any sense.

"I am keeping the baby," I told him. "If you feel you need to go, then go."

He told me he would try to stick around but would make no promises. I let out a long sigh. If he left, he left. I had made up my mind, and there was absolutely nothing Nate could say or do that would make me reconsider.

The lease on my apartment was coming to an end, and I was trying to position myself financially to prepare for the baby. Nate didn't have his own place at the time. He lived with friends, Thornton and Karen Chandler. They offered to let us both move in with them until we could decide what we wanted to do. Nate persuaded me that this was a good solution for our immediate future. He appealed to my practical side by pointing out that this would save money until we figured things out. I was still resigned to raising the baby on my own, so saving money in anticipation of the time I'd have to take off work was the right card for Nate to play.

The Chandlers had a decent-sized home and were sincere in their desire to help us, so I accepted. I put most items in storage, then moved my personal things in with Nate at the Chandlers' home. Things were cheerful for the first few days, and it was nice not to feel alone, but after that, Nate was almost never around. He would go away for days at a time and then show up with no explanation about where he had been. Then he disappeared for nearly three months. He called occasionally when he was in town for mini-camps, but he seemed uninterested in me or the baby. I was coming to terms with the fact that I was going to have this baby on my own. I cried. I prayed. I planned. I made a strict budget. I cried some more. It was a very dark time. Nate's rejection hurt me deeply.

I grew increasingly uncomfortable staying with the Chandlers. Even though they were always kind, I felt like an intruder. I was used to being independent. Nate was gone more than he was around, and this embarrassed me. I felt like a burden—and I didn't like the feeling. I didn't belong there with Nate's friends; I wasn't even sure I belonged with Nate. I started thinking about leasing an apartment on my own again.

I called my family, and they promised their support every step of the way. Friends from college and from church also came to see me and extended their love. These gestures reminded me that God still loved me. He hadn't given up on me—and neither should I give up on myself. Fortified by the love of family and friends, I decided to move into a place by myself.

One afternoon, the phone rang. It was Nate. "When I come back from camp," he said, "I want to know what the sex of the baby is."

"Why?" I asked. "What difference does that make?"

"Well, if it's a boy, then I'll try to work things out with you. If it's a girl, then I don't want to have anything to do with you," he said matter-of-factly.

I was horrified. *Was he serious?*

I had no idea what the sex of the baby was, but I felt my heart hardening. "Well, it's a girl," I said coldly, "so I guess when you get back from camp, you can just go on with your life, and I can go on with mine."

I fell into a routine of work, doctor appointments, and restless sleep. I stopped going to church. I was too ashamed to be pregnant and unmarried. It felt like anyone who looked at me was judging me, and it added weight to my shame. But even then, even in my doubts about the future, I was overwhelmed with love for this little child. I read books about pregnancy and children, wanting to learn all I could about being a good mother.

Football camp ended, and Nate called again. He wanted to know how I was doing and what the baby's due date was. He told me that during camp he spent time in deep reflection and had undergone a change of heart. There was compassion in his voice, and he seemed genuinely concerned about how I was feeling and how I was getting along during the pregnancy.

A few days later, Nate came to my apartment and apologized for his behavior and for being selfish—thinking more of how the baby affected him than me. He told me he was going to live up to his responsibilities and wanted us to raise the child together.

"Dot," he said, "I'm sorry, baby doll. I am truly sorry. I didn't mean to hurt you. I want to take care of you. I want to be with you. I want to take care of the baby. Please forgive me."

When I looked at him standing there, apologizing to me in earnest, my heart softened. I searched his eyes, looking for some sign that he meant what he said.

"I am going to take care of you," he said. "I will be here for you and the baby," he continued, "whether it's a boy or a girl."

I stood there, stroking my stomach and wanting so badly to be loved and cared for. I felt terribly alone. In my mind, I was already living in sin. My life was a chaotic mess. I knew living with a man was wrong, but what difference could it make now? I had already slept with him. I was pregnant with his child. Maybe letting him move in and take care of me was a good idea after all. At least I wouldn't be alone anymore.

"Alright," I said with a sigh.

Nate flashed his charismatic smile. "You'll see," he said. "Things will work out for us." He pulled me into an embrace, and for just a moment I stiffened, then relaxed and let him hold me. "I love you," he said. I was tired. I needed someone to love me, and Nate would do.

There was a shift in our relationship. By now I knew I was having a boy, but I didn't want to tell Nate. I wanted to see if he really wanted to be with me, regardless of the sex of the baby. He was calmer now. He had made the team again, and he wanted to spend time with me. He was gentle again and more like the man I had fallen in love with. *Did I only imagine the other things?* It seemed like I knew two completely different people — one was kind, funny, and attentive; the other was self-centered, brutish, and mean-spirited. *How could both of these be Nate?*

Wherever we went together, Nate was relaxed and completely at ease. He seemed ready to commit for the long term and genuinely excited to become a father. He was proud of me and introduced me as his wife, even to the media. I didn't correct him, but I didn't want to get married either. I wasn't sure how long the fair weather between us was going to last. Some part of me didn't believe Nate would stay around forever. I kept waiting for something to happen that would set off his anger and make him disappear again. I did finally tell him that the baby was a boy, and this made him very happy.

September came, and the days were beginning to shorten as the oppressive Texas heat at last lifted. I was having frequent dizzy spells and had become anemic. My doctor advised me to stop working. I was prepared. I had a good job and had always been frugal. I had saved and planned and always lived within my means, so I was covered. I didn't worry about things financially. Nate was around, but I didn't need him. It was important for me to be able to provide for myself.

⌒⌒

Football season was now in full swing. Even as I drew nearer to my due date, Nate insisted I come to all of the Cowboys games to watch him play. I went faithfully, but it wasn't as thrilling as it once had been. How I wished things were different. *If only I hadn't gotten pregnant*, I thought to myself. *What would things be like in my life right now?*

One Sunday night after a game, Nate was in an exceptionally good mood and asked me if I wanted to go with him to the state fair. He was in high spirits, and it sounded like fun. I was getting very close to my due date and feeling restless.

We went to the fair, and I ate anything and everything in sight. I just could not stop eating! Nate was making fun of me and seemed to be enjoying buying me more and more food. Before long I was totally miserable. I told him I wanted to just go home and rest. I had eaten too much and didn't feel well.

Nate took me back to the apartment and told me he was going to go out for a while but would check on me while he was gone. Just then, I felt a sensation like a needle pricking me in my right side. "Ouch!" I cried out.

Nate poked fun, "You just don't want me to leave, do you?"

"Go on," I said, "get out of here!" and I meant it. I was so full of food I didn't care if he came or went — I just wanted to lie down. There it was again. "Ouch!" It felt like a needle jabbing me. *Why did I eat so much?*

Nate came back a little later, and I felt the sticking pain again. He decided to hang around just in case I needed him. The needle pricks kept returning. It didn't seem to fit the description of any labor pains I had heard of or read about, but I decided to call the doctor just in case. While I was on the phone with my physician, it happened twice more, and he told me to come in immediately: I was in labor.

We drove from Coppell to Medical City in Dallas. On the way there, I could not seem to get comfortable. I kept squirming around in my seat, and then it felt like someone was jabbing me in my side with a needle. When I arrived, the medical team examined me, and I was already dilated. Within one hour, Nathaniel Newton III (Tré) was born.

On October 15, 1989, God blessed me with a beautiful baby boy. It was the most precious gift I had ever received. For the first time in months, I felt the sun come out in my soul. I was deliriously happy as I held that little bundle in my arms. It was a turning point.

God revealed himself to me there in my hospital room. I felt him whisper my name. I felt him wash away my sin and shame. I knew I would love this little boy for the rest of my life. As surely as I knew I would never leave this little baby, I knew God would never leave me. As much as I knew that little boy could never do anything that would make me stop loving him, I knew God would love me forever, no matter what. I understood God's love was perfect, and there was nothing I could do to cause him to take it away from me. It was like receiving a warm embrace—I felt God again, and it felt good.

The whole hospital seemed to celebrate. Nate Newton just had a baby boy—a son! He pranced around the hospital cracking jokes and shaking everyone's hand. He bought pizza for the entire floor. Nate was on top of the world. He had a son! I was lying in my room, thinking, *Wow, he's really happy!* Then, just as soon as that thought came, another took its place: *I wonder how long this will last.*

It was almost like I wasn't even there — the whole place was buzzing around Nate, congratulating him, slapping him on the back, asking for autographs. I was just part of the background scenery, but I didn't care. I had Tré. Tré was the world to me now. I looked into his eyes, and I melted. No matter what happened with Nate, I would have this child to love. That was enough.

I had prayed for this little baby every day, no matter how sad I felt or how much fear, doubt, and shame I experienced. I prayed he would embrace the reality that he is God's son. I looked at my little boy, and tears welled up in my eyes. One of the nurses expressed concern that I seemed so sad. She didn't understand. I felt like I had a chance to make things right in my life again. It was like turning over a new page with no mistakes on it. I knew Tré was special. I was proud to be his mother. I was overwhelmed that God had trusted me with his life. I kept quoting the prophet Samuel: "For this child I prayed; and the LORD hath given me my petition which I asked of him: Therefore also I have lent him to the LORD; as long as he liveth he shall be lent to the LORD" (1 Samuel 1:27 – 28).

"O God, I love you," I whispered. "I can feel how much you love me. Thank you. Thank you for giving me this peace. Thank you for giving me something so wonderful in the midst of something so bad. Thank you for this baby boy."

The tears kept softly flowing, but they were not tears of sadness; they were tears of release. Several nurses hovered nearby, and as they checked my vital signs, they were concerned at my tears. All I could say to them was, "I'm overwhelmed with love."

CHAPTER 16

Ups and Downs

I am so accustomed to being
unstable that the only stability
in my life is being unstable.

Josh Lucas

The six weeks following Tré's birth were beautiful. My family came to help out with the baby, and I found a great deal of comfort in spending time alone with God and Tré. I pushed it to the back of my mind that I was living with Nate in an unmarried relationship. I was focused on taking care of Tré. Feeling God's presence again in my life was so fulfilling that I didn't want to deal with anything that might hinder the reconnection I felt. I knew I would have to deal with it sooner or later, but later was better.

December came, and Nate and I shared another birthday. But the next day it was like someone had flipped a switch. Nate was a different person again. He started coming in late at night, or not at all. He was drinking more, and his language became increasingly coarse. Sometimes he came in at two or three in the morning and demanded that I get up and fix him something to eat—and not just a sandwich; he wanted a complete meal. I was exhausted from taking care of the baby, but to refuse him meant an argument, and I didn't want him to wake up Tré. Once or twice he grabbed me hard and shoved me against the wall. It frightened me. Nate had always had a temper, but he had never physically hurt me before. I told myself we were all just really tired from taking care of a newborn.

I still had one more month of maternity leave, and I was trying to figure out child care. The thought of leaving Tré with someone else terrified me, but the thought of becoming financially dependent on Nate terrified me even more. Nate's early morning rants were bringing up very bad memories, and I was determined not to find myself in the same position my mother had been. I wanted to keep my job; Nate wanted me to stay home with his son. We argued about it, but my arguments were halfhearted because I agreed with Nate—I wanted to stay home with Tré. I wanted to take care of him. I wanted to protect him. I wanted to raise him.

I turned in my resignation. I had saved enough money that if I was careful, I could live for up to a year without needing a penny from Nate. This gave me comfort. For the first two weeks following my resignation, Nate was thrilled that I had decided to stay home with Tré. In short order, however, he began complaining that I was dependent on him. He grew irritable, argumentative, and insulting. The Cowboys were not playing well, which made his mood even blacker. The season ended early, leaving Nate with lots of free time and few obligations. He'd disappear for several days at a time, then reappear as if he had just stepped out for milk.

There was no commitment; we just sort of acted married whenever it suited Nate. He still loved to go on road trips and loved showing off Tré. By the time Tré was four months old, we were taking trips as long as three weeks at a time to visit family members and friends in Louisiana, Florida, North Carolina, and Georgia. I didn't mind because things were good when we traveled. He beamed with pride whenever he introduced Tré to someone.

I was developing new clarity about my relationship with Nate. My role was to drop everything and make myself available to him whenever he needed me. Whenever he didn't need me, I receded into the background to wait patiently until he needed me again. He didn't treat me badly, but the time he spent with me wasn't about loving me or being with me; it was about Tré.

He was proud of having a son, and I was his son's mother. I didn't have freedom to make plans on my own because I always needed to be available whenever Nate called. Wherever we went, Nate introduced me as his wife. People naturally assumed we were married. We acted married. We had a son. I think even our closest friends had just assumed all along that we were married. I often felt like Nate and I were strangers.

It was October 1990. I had been at home with Tré for a year and was seriously considering returning to work. However, I had promised Nate that I would not go back to my career until Tré was at least two. When my lease came up, I had to decide if life with Nate was "good enough" to maintain. *What did I want? What else would I do if I left him?* Sometimes I looked in the mirror and saw my mother staring back at me, but I shrugged it off. Our relationship wasn't like that of my mother and stepfather. Nate didn't beat me. I could leave if I wanted to.

When my lease expired, it was up to Nate to decide what to do. Since I didn't have a job, finding a place to live was his decision. I didn't feel like I should weigh in much, since I couldn't contribute financially. He had often talked about having a house with a yard for Tré to play in, and a house sounded nice to me. There was a little place Nate was interested in near Coppell Deli, a favorite stop for the players on the way to the airport for away games. The house was small and in much need of repair, but this didn't matter to me. I wanted Nate to understand that I was with him because I loved him and because we had a child together. People called our place "Newton's Shack" and poked fun at it, but it never bothered me. It seemed to please Nate that I didn't care about money. He was satisfied that I loved him for who he was and not because of his celebrity status.

We moved into the tiny house, and I went to work making it a home for Nate, Tré, and me. I was like a domestic goddess—running all the errands, cooking, washing, ironing, packing his bags. I even got involved in scheduling his appearances and researching his endorsements. I was now totally financially dependent on him, and he was totally emotionally dependent on me. He was used to having me at his beck and call. But it wasn't long before things got worse between us again. Nate stayed out late all the time and didn't communicate his plans. A woman accused him of fathering her child. He denied it flatly, but he had hired an attorney. I never had any proof, but I was always suspicious he had paid her off. I knew he was sleeping around—many of the players were; it was part of the life.

Nate spent more and more time in clubs and on the streets. He would roll in at 3:00 or 4:00 a.m., demanding full-course meals. If I refused, he threatened me or hurled profanities. I usually found myself doing whatever he asked just to appease him. One night, Nate stayed out all night and came home at noon the next day. Finally I'd had enough. I was tired of being disrespected. I was tired of being yelled at. I was tired of the other women. I told him I couldn't live like that anymore and asked him to put a deposit on an apartment so I could move out. He cursed at me and yelled, "You're not going anywhere!"

He moved close to me in a hot rage, and I was scared. I thought he might actually hit me this time, so I went into another room. Satisfied that he had won the argument, Nate got undressed to take a nap. I decided I would wait until he was asleep, and then I'd run out of the house. The only problem was that he was in the bedroom, so I couldn't grab any clothes to take with me.

As soon as I was sure he had nodded off, I went out to my car and put nine-month-old Tré into his car seat. I was leaving for good. But when I put the key into the ignition, Nate came running out of the house wearing only his underwear.

"Where are you going?" he shouted. "You better not leave!"

I put the car in gear to back out, and in a split second, Nate crashed his fist into the windshield, shattering it on the driver's side. I screamed.

Our driveway was in plain sight of a busy street. People stopped and looked, but no one called the police or attempted to intervene. I was terrified. I backed out of the driveway, shaking, glass shattered on the seat and in my lap and Tré crying loudly. *Where should I go?*

I drove to a nearby park and sat there in shock. *Who should I call? Who would believe that Nate could do such a thing?* I had met a lot of Nate's teammates and their families, but I didn't really know any of them.

I thought about calling Lynn Martin. She had spent enough time with us to know Nate didn't always treat me well. In fact, we'd been at their house one night when Nate dropped a bomb on all of us. K-Mart had turned to Nate and said, "Hey, Time [*Big Time* was K-Mart's nickname for Nate], you got you a son!"

"Yeah," Nate replied, "that's my baby boy alright, but I got me another son too."

Lynn, K-Mart, and I just looked at each other stunned, but none of us said anything to Nate. Later on, I questioned Nate and learned he had a son he had never seen but was paying child support for. It was on his mind that night because the woman wanted her new husband to adopt the boy, and Nate had to sign papers so the adoption could proceed.

I felt like Lynn would understand how afraid I was that Nate had gotten angry enough to damage property. But I also knew that Lynn had little tolerance for sadness or excuses of any kind. If I told her a problem, she would speak praises over me, remind me of my destiny, and tell me who I needed to be. I imagined that if I shared with her, she would look at me with concern, but her response would likely be, "You're a strong woman. You can get through this."

Nevertheless, I put the car in gear and started to drive to her house. Then I realized that telling Lynn was definitely not going to work. I was afraid of what she would tell her husband—and I couldn't imagine what would happen if Nate found out I had exposed his violent temper to Lynn and K-Mart.

I called Sheila, my former roommate. When she cheerfully answered the phone, I wavered. She was with her new husband and sounded so happy. I knew if I told her what had happened, she would drop everything and come to my rescue, but I just couldn't spoil her happiness. I hung up the phone and stared through my broken windshield. *What now?*

I had rushed out of the house quickly and had nothing with me but Tré and my purse. I decided I would spend the night in a hotel and go back to the house the next day to get some things before leaving for good. Then reality set in. I had no place to stay and no job. My mother's face flashed before my eyes, and I shuddered. *How had I let this happen to me?* I had no choice but to go back to Nate. Then I could begin looking for a job so I could prepare to leave.

I went back to the little house the next day, preparing for the worst, but Nate came home like a flipped coin. He was a completely different person. He apologized and said he was so ashamed of himself. He begged me not to leave. I told him I would stay, but I was going to get a job. He pleaded with me to think of our son and not go back to work. *Stick with the plan*, I thought. But he brought up God and said all the right things. I told him I wanted him to take me home to Louisiana so I could see my mom. I planned to tell her what was going on so we could figure out what to do. And maybe I would just stay there with her and not even come back.

Nate felt so bad about what had happened that he agreed to take me to Louisiana, but he made sure I was never out of his sight. As usual, he painted himself to be the good guy, treating everyone to dinner and handing out money until they were all under his spell. For the three days we were there, it was like I was wearing a leash attached to Nate. He never left me alone for one minute. I quickly gave up all hope of talking to someone. I knew it wasn't going to happen, and no one in my family had even the faintest clue that he was mistreating me. To them Nate was a hero and a gentleman, and I was his lucky celebrity wife, someone to be envied, not pitied.

When we left Louisiana, instead of heading west back to Dallas, Nate started driving south. We ended up in Orlando to visit his family and friends. I did my best to fake good spirits, but I was miserable. Like a broken record, I couldn't stop replaying the mistakes of the last year. One bad choice (to go on the pill) led to another bad choice (to have sex), which led to a bad situation (being pregnant and not married), which led to another bad choice (live with Nate, leave my job, etc.). *If only I could go back in time and fix the first mistake!* One decision had led me down a detour of winding, bumpy, difficult roads — away from my dreams, away from my destiny. I felt trapped.

We spent three weeks on the road traveling from place to place and visiting people. Along the way, we talked about what had happened, and Nate assured me that things would be different when we got home. He promised to get control of his drinking and his temper. He grew attentive again. He was kind when he spoke to me, and once again things improved between us. I let my guard down and started to think that maybe we had turned a corner.

Everywhere I went, people were starstruck with Nate Newton. The moment they knew I was his "wife" (at least they all believed I was his wife), out came the special treatment. Even at church, people often brought me items and asked me to take them home for Nate or other Cowboys players to autograph. It was frustrating. Instead of being interested in me, it seemed like belonging to Nate was the most interesting thing about me. I was losing who I was. My whole world was wrapped up in Nate.

CHAPTER 17

Settling

The first and worst of all frauds is to cheat
one's self. All sin is easy after that.

Pearl Bailey

Lies have a way of compounding, like interest on credit card debt. Before long, you are totally engulfed, and it is hard to distinguish the truth from falsehood. I knew Nate was cheating on me, and it was increasingly difficult for me to be intimate with him. He always denied it, but he stayed out late all the time and sometimes didn't come home until the next day. Sometimes when he had too much to drink, he emptied his pockets and a scrap of paper would fall out with a woman's phone number or address scrawled on it. I scooped them up, determined to learn who he had been with.

A friend of mine and her husband had come into town and came over for a visit. She wanted to know all about the lifestyle of being married to a professional athlete (even my friends thought we were married because Nate always referred to me as his wife in the media). I looked her straight in the eyes and told her Nate was cheating on me and that I wanted to leave him.

"Do you know for sure?" she asked.

"No. I don't have proof, if that's what you mean, but I *know* he is cheating. I have something I want to check out. Will you go with me?" I asked.

She was reluctant, but I didn't want to go alone, and I persuaded her to tag along. We went to an address on a piece of paper that fell out of Nate's pocket one drunken night. Jackpot! Nate was actually there! Not only was he there; he was sitting outside, snuggling up with the woman in plain sight. I had suspected this all along, but seeing it with my own eyes was still a shock.

Reality set in, and I saw red. I made a scene so he would know I was there and then took my friend back to her husband. Afterward, I felt terrible. Not only was I disgusted with Nate, but I was upset for dragging my friend through the ordeal. I didn't know what else to do but apologize to her. I was truly sorry I had involved her.

When I got back home, Nate was waiting for me. He begged for my forgiveness, but I was too angry to give it to him. I pleaded with him to give me enough money for an apartment and day care—just until I could get on my feet, and then I would never bother him again. I just wanted to leave. He obviously didn't want me, so why should I stay?

Out came Nate's broken record, playing the same old tune, but this time he added a new note: "Everyone has always abandoned me, Dot. I need you. You are the only person in my life I can count on—the only one who has never let me down, has never left me. I need your help. You *can't* leave me."

My heart was hardened. In the moment, I might have told him he was forgiven, but I certainly didn't mean it. Instead, I started planning. I had received payment for some of my work scheduling Nate's appearances and endorsements and I was expecting an income tax refund of $1,400. It wasn't much, but I was going to use the money to get out. I knew it would be four to six weeks before the check came, which was enough time to find a cheap and decent day care for Tré while I found a job.

For weeks, I kept an eye out for that tax refund. It was time to escape. When I went to the mailbox and finally saw an envelope from the IRS, my heart skipped a beat. I ran back into the house and tore it open, but there was no check inside. Instead, there was a notice saying the refund I was expecting had gone to pay property taxes in my name—and I owed an additional $700! I felt crushed by disappointment. Stuck again!

I had no knowledge about the property. When I called my mother to ask about it, she said she did have property in my name, but she had definitely paid the taxes. There was no way to clear it up quickly; it was going to take some time to sort out. I had no choice but to tell Nate and ask for his help. He graciously paid the remaining balance, and I thanked God that Nate was willing to help, but I was still unhappy that I was financially dependent on him. I decided it was time to position myself for independence. It was time to get a job.

While Nate was in training camp, I secured a job at First Coppell Bank. Time went by, and Nate and I came to terms with things. We found a place of happiness. I was more at ease because I was earning an income, so I didn't feel trapped anymore. I could stay, or I could leave. But I couldn't shake my guilt about living together and not being married, so I started praying about our relationship. I looked back over the past ten months and realized that things had been calm and even. In fact, things were good. I enjoyed being with Nate. He was a good father to Tré. I had no more excuses not to marry him.

I approached Nate about getting married, and he was open to it. I told him I had been spending a lot of time in prayer and that I could no longer continue living together with him in sin. I told him that if the way things were between us now was the real deal, then I would be happy to become his wife.

My objection to marrying Nate had been because he wasn't saved. Nate reminded me that he still wasn't a Christian. I knew this, but he always encouraged my walk with the Lord, and I attributed Nate's lack of devotion to his hectic football schedule. I told myself that when football was over for him, he would accept Christ once and for all. The new year was fast approaching, and I wanted to start if off right.

PART 4

A Troubled Marriage

CHAPTER 18

I Do ...

Between a man and his wife
nothing ought to rule but love.

William Penn

D o you, Nathaniel Newton Jr., take this woman, Dorothy Johnson, to be your lawfully wedded wife?" asked the justice of the peace.

"I do," Nate answered.

"Do you, Dorothy Johnson, take this man, Nathaniel Newton Jr., to be your lawfully wedded husband?"

"I do."

After a couple of years spent living together, we were married in a simple courthouse ceremony. T. Hayes stood up with Nate, and Sheila stood up with me. We sent announcements to all of our friends, and everyone was shocked — they thought we had been married since Tré was born.

Nineteen ninety-two was a good year for us. The Cowboys won the Super Bowl at the end of the 1992 season, and Nate went on to play in the Pro Bowl. We spent lots of time together, just the three of us. Nate communicated with me differently now, and I felt more secure. At Easter, he was asked to speak at church, and he surprised me by saying yes! He encouraged me to spend time with the Lord and be active in church. Whenever I asked him to come to church with me, he was always clear that he had too much respect for God to play with him. He'd say, "When I get myself completely together, I'll start going to church. Right now, I'm just not good enough."

In the fall of 1992, the new season had begun, and the Dallas Cowboys were off to a great start. They were winning almost every game, and with every victory, the media focused more attention on Nate. He was their darling. He always gave an entertaining interview, and there wasn't a sports station on television that didn't want their moment with him. He had more opportunities for endorsements and appearances than ever before. He had become a hot item overnight.

I was very busy scheduling appearances for Nate, making sure he was always prepared, packing for him, and attending both home and away games. I had quit my job at Coppell Bank in October because taking care of Nate was a full-time endeavor during the week. On the weekends, I was responsible for entertaining family and guests. The more attention Nate received, the more the old Nate surfaced. Once again, he started drinking too much and coming home late — if he came home at all. When he did show up, he demanded meals or sex. The more this old pattern emerged, the more fearful I grew. *This cannot be happening again; we just got married!* I reminded him of his promise that things would be different.

"Dot," he said, "I'm not perfect, but I promise to do the right things. If you wanted a perfect husband, you shouldn't have married me."

We argued constantly, and his temper grew increasingly violent. He sometimes shoved me or grabbed my throat when he was angry, but he always apologized later. He was drinking all the time. I knew he was drinking and driving, but if I expressed any concerns, it started an argument, and the arguments were physically violent. Once he'd crossed that line, it was easier and easier for him to do. The abuse got worse.

Nate had a routine. On Wednesday, he went to work. Later, he'd call to see if he had an appearance and, if so, at what time. If there was nothing on his schedule, he'd tell me what he wanted me to cook or pick up for him and when I should have it ready. He'd usually arrive home around 7:00 p.m., eat dinner, and then watch movies in his media room until he fell asleep.

Thursdays were much the same, only it was more likely he had an appearance. He usually wanted Tré and me to be present at all his appearances. We were rarely on camera, but he wanted us to be there supporting him.

On Friday before a game, he stayed home or came home early. He would invite people into town to see the game, and it was my job to entertain them. He would be jolly on Friday night, looking good and being gregarious. By Saturday morning, he would be detoxing and treating me like a servant. People stayed with us every weekend there was a home game, and I was supposed to keep all of his guests out of his way. I also had to make sure Tré made absolutely no noise, fix Nate exactly what he wanted to eat, and serve it when he wanted it.

On Saturday afternoons before a game, the Cowboys sequestered their players in a hotel to keep them out of trouble. Whether the game was home or away, the Cowboys made sure their players were all safely tucked into a hotel where they could keep an eye on their assets. Then I could relax a little — but not much. I knew at some point Nate would call from the hotel and demand that I drop whatever I was doing to bring him food or his music or anything else he wanted.

On Sunday mornings of home games, he would come home from the hotel, no matter what time the game started. I had to make sure the house was kept in complete silence and that no one disturbed him. I wasn't supposed to do anything but be in the room with him, keeping everything perfect. He didn't want the phones to ring or Tré to bother him, and he always asked, "Did you pray for me?" Sundays were stressful.

On his way to the game, Nate would call me with his ticket

list. He loved to get tickets for people, but he liked waiting until the very last minute before deciding to give the tickets away. I was then supposed to contact everyone and organize everything. It was my responsibility to see to it that his guests arrived comfortably at the game and that I was there with Tré as well.

It was impossible to make it through the weekend without angering him in some way. T. Hayes would call to give me a heads-up if he knew Nate was angry with me. "I talked to that boy," he'd say, "and I can tell he's not gonna be in a good mood." T. Hayes knew what was going on. If things were really bad, I would call and tell him Nate was hurting me. I sometimes asked him, "Why don't you talk to Nate?"

"Nate's trying, Dot," he said. "I don't know what's wrong with that boy."

We always went out to eat with family and friends after the game. After we came home, he'd spend an hour drilling me on every play. I had to pay close attention during the game and not get distracted visiting with other wives, or I'd be in trouble. Then it was time for Nate to hit the streets. Sometimes he came back late that night, and sometimes he didn't. Whenever he did get home, there would be an argument. I tried my hardest to ignore it, but that didn't work very often. I knew he would come home sometime, insisting I make him food or have sex—and I didn't want to give him either. I started to hate him.

At the end of the 1993 season, the Cowboys won another Super Bowl championship. I worked as Nate's local agent, scheduling appearances and endorsements and reviewing contracts for commercials. This was now my full-time job. Tré and I attended most of the appearances to watch him sign autographs or appear on television or commercials, but in between we rarely saw him. He turned cold and distant.

One night, Nate grabbed me by the hair and pulled me around the house. I wanted to call the police, but I just knew it wouldn't make any difference. Nate always got out of trouble as quickly as he got into it. He could charm his way out of anything.

Nate spent lots of money on people and was always the life of the party. He gave liberally to my family, including vehicles as well as cash. They all loved him, but it made things worse for me. If one of them made him mad, he took it out on me. If I tried to keep him from giving them things (because it would eventually blow back on me), my family got angry with me. They didn't understand and thought I was being selfish, trying to keep Nate from sharing with them.

Then a close friend of mine came to me one day, telling me that Nate had come to her apartment, coming on to her for sex. When I confronted Nate about it, he threatened me, abused me, and choked me. I knew she was telling the truth, but Nate accused her of coming on to him.

I felt isolated and alone. I desperately wanted help, and part of me wanted to confide in someone, but several things stopped me. First, my friend Lynn was leaving. K-Mart had signed with the Seattle Seahawks, and they were moving to Washington. Telling her seemed pointless. *How could she help from Seattle?* Plus, each time Nate abused me, I convinced myself it would be the last time. It sometimes felt like I had done something wrong and that when I had been sufficiently punished, the abuse would stop. I was also genuinely afraid that if I went to someone about Nate, they might confront him and make things worse for me. Finally, I believed that if I had to go through all of this in order for Nate to receive Christ, then I was willing to live through it and pay that price.

So, I told no one. Just God. I cried all of my tears in silence. I poured out my grief and believed I was suffering as a result of my own bad choices, that I somehow deserved this treatment because of my mistakes. Someday I would pay it all back, and this hard part would be over.

I lived two completely separate lives. One life was inside my home — frightened, abused, angry, and alone. The other life was outside my home — a functional, normal celebrity wife. I remember watching the other wives and wondering about their lives. *Were they happy? Were their husbands faithful? Did they struggle with abuse like I did, or were their homes peaceful? Did other celebrity wives go through abuse too, or was there just something wrong with my life?*

I couldn't wait for the season to be over. I wanted to disappear. It was getting harder and harder to hide the physical abuse, but I knew I had to. If anyone had an inkling of what was really going on, I believed Nate would have killed me.

After the Super Bowl, the Pro Bowl came around, and we went with Nate to Hawaii. For once, he was completely relaxed, and I didn't have to worry about extra people, appearances, schedules, or endorsements. It was the nicest time I'd experienced in years.

When we returned home, the public appearances started up again, and so did Nate's antics. Now he was constantly in trouble — with women, DUIs, and general bad behavior. In no time at all, he'd gone from media darling to media bad boy. As the press attention turned negative, his reputation suffered. The worse it got in the media, the more he took it out on me. There were times he beat me until I was unable to move. The abuse was happening more frequently, and it was getting more violent. The morning after a beating, Nate would either act as if nothing had happened the night before, or he would be extremely nice to me. I hated my roller-coaster life. I never knew from one moment to the next what to expect from Nate Newton. Sometimes I thought I would go to sleep and it would be my last moment alive.

The Cowboys continued to do well, and I was extremely busy taking care of Nate and his calendar. The arguments and beatings never stopped, so I just accepted it as part of life. Whenever he was upset, he abused me. Then he would apologize and want to "make things right." Each time I thought, *This is the last thing I'll have to go through.* And of course I was always wrong. I know it sounds crazy, but I honestly thought I deserved the abusive treatment as punishment for my sins.

I never knew how much money Nate had, and I never cared. I knew he spent lots and lots of money — he had an obsession with cars and dogs — but he didn't spend it on me. He used only one credit card, American Express. The bill went to his agent in Florida each month, so I had no idea how much he spent or what he spent it on. I received enough money from him each month to pay our household bills, and he paid me for organizing his events and appearances. Since I wasn't allowed to have many friends or hang out with other Cowboys wives, I didn't need much money.

On one occasion, he had so overspent that his agent forwarded the American Express bill to the house for Nate to review. I saw this bill, including charges to Louis Vuitton and fine jewelry stores. Of course, none of these items were for me. But I wondered about the woman he had purchased them for. I wondered if she knew about me. I never shopped lavishly, and any spending money I received had come from my modest salary at First Coppell Bank and now from scheduling Nate's appearances. I knew that if I had asked for something, Nate would have given it to me. He was generous with everybody. But I didn't want to ask.

One Thursday night, I was sitting in the passenger seat of Nate's truck, and we were arguing about that credit card bill. I asked him about the charges and who the items were for. Without warning, he hit me in the face over my left eye.

"It's my money, b_____! You better not ever question me. You have no right to question me about how I spend my money, who I spend it on, where I spend it. Just because you're my wife doesn't give you a reason to question my business!"

The blow left a visible bruise. I knew I couldn't miss a game without serious consequences from Nate, so I wore big sunglasses and went to the stadium. Sandy Irvin came over, and after she was done loving on Tré, she said, "Dot, can I tell you something?" I looked up at her, wondering if she could see my bruise. Fear gripped me. *Can she tell? Can she see it?* I felt the lowest I had ever been.

"Dot, you are a beautiful person," Sandy said. "You are just so beautiful!" I wanted to burst into tears. It was as if God had sent her to me to remind me that he loved me.

Every time I summoned the courage to leave Nate or go to the authorities, it seemed like he got into trouble with the law. I told myself I needed to stay and see him through whatever crisis he was in—and then I would go. Each time I stuck with him, he would be grateful, and things would get better for a little while.

I still felt responsible for Nate's spiritual condition—that it was my assignment to see him through to salvation. After a beating, I would think, *This is the last thing I'll have to go through, and then it will be good. If it means Nate will come to know the Lord, this will all be worth it.* I rationalized that I was keeping the worst of it hidden from Tré, and so I was the only one paying a price. When things started to heat up, I would send Tré to play in his room, or I'd start a movie for him. I never wanted him to be frightened. I knew Nate would never ever hurt Tré. I just wished he felt the same about me.

By the end of 1994, I was completely exhausted—mentally, emotionally, and physically. I didn't have the strength for one more argument or one more beating. I just wanted it to end. One night after Nate had pushed me around, cursed, and yelled at me for hours, I poured out all my sorrow and grief to God. "Lord, I'm ready to be with you," I prayed. "I don't care if I live or die."

I hugged my knees to my chest, wishing for one moment that I might die then and there so I could be safe with God forever. Then, in the same moment, I suddenly wanted Tré to know this same love I had for God—how I felt like he was hugging me through all these painful times.

"God, let me live," I whispered. "Let me live so I can teach Tré to love you like I do." In that moment, more than anything, I wanted to live. I wanted to survive, so I could be the one to teach Tré to love God with all his heart, soul, and mind. I wanted him to grow up strong and healthy and become a godly man. It didn't matter what else I had to go through if it meant that Tré had what he needed.

CHAPTER 19

The Good Life

Success makes life easier.
It doesn't make living easier.

Bruce Springsteen

As the 1994 season began, the Cowboys were coming off back-to-back Super Bowl championships and were at their peak. Nate was in his prime as a professional athlete and had grown wealthy. So when Nate spotted a rat one night at our modest home in Coppell, that was it—it was time to move! Nate decided he wanted to build his own home. He wanted land and privacy—a respite from everything that had to do with the Dallas Cowboys.

Nate put me in charge of getting the house built. He wanted to pay for everything with cash—no mortgage, no debt. As long as I stayed within the budget and the house was comfortable for entertaining, Nate trusted me to take care of all the details. It was one of the nicest things Nate ever did for me.

It was wonderful to have the freedom to make decisions. Planning and working with the builder made me feel important, and I enjoyed the process. Nate never once complained about any decisions I made or the furniture I chose. He seemed genuinely excited as the house took shape, and he enjoyed listening to me ramble on and on about the details of the build. Focusing on the project was a good diversion, and for the most part, things went well between us.

We had a wonderful builder, and he was around often enough to see us in unguarded moments when things were not so nice between Nate and me. He never witnessed any outright physical abuse, but he seemed to know that things were not all they appeared to be, and he was especially gentle and kind with me.

The only blowup Nate and I had about the house happened when the builders made a mistake with the front of the house. I wanted it to be a certain way, but the builders did something else. I decided I could live with it, but when Nate found out about it, he was livid. He did not want me to settle for what had happened. We scheduled a meeting with our builder, but before going in, Nate threatened me that I better fix this. In other words, I had to insist they fix it exactly like I wanted it in the first place without any change in the price. I was horrified. I didn't want to make a fuss with the builders, but I also didn't want to make Nate angry. I went into the meeting to discuss the problem, but before the meeting was over, I was yelling. I felt so terrible about the whole thing. As I left the meeting, I asked God to forgive me and hoped that the men would somehow understand that the person they saw wasn't who I really was. I was upset about it for days afterward.

Just as the house was finished and we were ready to move in, it was time for Tré to begin kindergarten. Even though Fort Worth Christian School was an hour-long drive from the new house, it was important to me to keep Tré there. I wanted him to be in a Christian environment that reinforced the values I was teaching him at home. It was a good school—and the right one for Tré. I didn't mind the drive at all, because being away from home was good for me too.

My best friend from college, Sheila, was in the process of moving to Atlanta, and I knew I was going to miss her. I was making new friends at Tré's school, but as usual, most people were interested in becoming my friend more because I was

Nate Newton's wife and less because I was Dorothy. But within a week of school starting, I met Ingrid at Tré's Tae Kwon Do class. She noticed people flopping all over me, bringing me things for Nate to autograph or wanting to talk about football, and she kept her distance. I noticed her because she was not seeking me out, so I introduced myself to her. We were about to throw a birthday party for Tré at Texas Stadium with five hundred people in attendance. When I invited Ingrid, she was shocked since I didn't really know her. But I sensed she was genuine, and I believed we would become friends. We started driving to Tae Kwon Do tournaments together, and before long, we became very close friends.

Nate was gone a lot, and Ingrid's husband, Monte, was an executive who worked long hours. When our kids were in school, Ingrid and I had more time to spend together. We would do her errands together one day, and then do my errands together the next day. We exercised together, did Bible study together, and went to school functions and our children's special events together. I loved being with her. Little by little, I began to open up to her about my life — the good and the bad.

Ingrid listened to me with such patience and gentleness. She listened to me talk about the abuse, and I must have sounded like a broken record, but she listened to me every time like it was the first time she had ever heard me. When Nate would apologize and promise that things would be better, I would tell Ingrid he had turned a corner, and she listened. Then, when things would get bad again and the abuse would start over, she listened and never judged me. She validated who I was and promised to stand with me and do whatever it took. I made her promise to never say anything to her husband, and she swore she never would.

Ingrid and I talked every day, but I didn't always tell her

when things were bad. Sometimes it was just good to get up, get out of the house, and have someone to be with who loved me and treated me well. I didn't want to spoil things all the time by complaining about life with Nate. Ingrid always allowed me to be myself. I could not imagine my life without her in it. Ingrid was just like family.

⌐⌐

In the fall of 1994, Nate got into trouble with the law. He'd been in a car accident while under the influence of alcohol. After pleading guilty to reckless conduct, he received a six-month probation sentence. Once again, this brought negative press attention and a public trial, but I stood by him, supporting him and offering encouragement. This touched Nate. He knew I was sincere in my support, and he really did try to adjust his behavior and become a better husband through the ordeal. He spent more and more time at home, and things were calm between us. Nate even agreed to see a counselor with me.

We began asking around, and someone from the Cowboys recommended a counselor. It turned out to be a complete waste of time—the man seemed bored in the session, and I swore there were times he actually dozed off. We went to two sessions and then quit. Things were pretty good between us again, so it didn't seem like we even needed a counselor. Plus, Nate was more open to church now, though he had still not given his life to Christ. But he sometimes spoke with ministers and seemed to be making positive changes in his behavior. I was happy that things were calm and that he seemed to be making progress, but I remained uneasy. I couldn't relax. I had given up hope that things would ever really be permanently good. I was always waiting for something bad to happen.

It was difficult for me to trust people. When someone

reached out to me for friendship, it seemed they were more intrigued by Nate's public persona. I would visit with someone and go to lunch, but the conversation always turned to football. It was like this even at church. People constantly brought me photos and other items and asked me to take them home for Nate or other Cowboys players to sign. I still went to services, but I started to sneak in after the service started and slipped out just before it ended. I continued to attend regularly, but I felt disconnected—like a spectator. I was hurt that people's interest in me was all about Nate, so I began to withdraw.

Once, during a time when things were bad, I went to a minister and told him I was in danger. He immediately began making excuses for Nate, telling me that most of what I was experiencing was probably a result of the unique issues a celebrity has to deal with. Without missing a breath, he then turned the conversation back to football. He seemed very pleased with himself. I didn't even need to be in the room; he carried on the whole conversation by himself. I sat there listening, wondering if he had any idea how much courage it took for me to even think about coming to him with my problems.

Meanwhile, Nate continued to make forward progress. He had always loved to read. He read almost every night before he went to bed, and he began to read more often from the Bible. I was very encouraged by this. He began spending time with the Dallas Cowboys chaplain as well. Nate would come home excited after talking with him and share the highlights of their conversations with me. He didn't go into great detail about his personal relationship with God, but his actions spoke louder than his words ever could have.

Nate was changing. He was living a life that was pleasing to God, and he was better toward me. It had been a long time since there had been any physical abuse, and Nate began talking about wanting another child, reminding me that I had always said I wanted two. I was not ready for this. Too many times, I had been up and down on the Nate Newton roller coaster, and I was still holding my breath for the next frightening drop. I couldn't even think about complicating things by bringing another baby into the picture.

Nate's behavior was steadily improving, but he still had occasional relapses. He was charged with a misdemeanor assault, accused of fondling a woman in a bar. He was found not guilty, and the matter was dropped. There were no repercussions from this at home, and the rest of 1995 came and went without incident. The Cowboys had won another Super Bowl, and Nate had gone to the Pro Bowl again. Throughout that year, Nate had been gentle with me. He was more responsive to Tré and seemed to be consistently working to improve himself and become a better man.

We spent time together in prayer and fellowship with some church leaders from Tré's school. Nate asked me to forgive him for his rocky past and for how he had treated me. I struggled with fear and doubt, but I did forgive Nate. I opened up my heart and asked God to give me the strength to see Nate as he was meant to be, not as he had been. I wanted to give Nate a chance to truly change.

CHAPTER 20

A New Day

Though no one can go back and make a
brand-new start, anyone can start from
now and make a brand-new ending.

Carl Bard

It was now 1996, and Nate was better than ever. He came to me one day, held my hand, and apologized. He told me he knew he had done a lot of wrong things to me in the past—terrible things, unthinkable and inexcusable things. He told me I didn't deserve to be treated that way—that I had never deserved to be treated that way. He brought up all the times I stood by him when I could have walked away and told me it meant a great deal to him.

"Dot, I'm sorry," he said, holding my hands tightly and looking me right in the eyes. "I'm so sorry. I love you, and I have changed. I know I tell you all the time I'm not perfect, but this time, instead of telling you I'm not perfect, I'm telling you I want to be who God wants me to be. I want you to help me become that man. You have been through enough. Dot, I'm sorry. You have to believe me . . ."

I had forgiven him, and things had been good between us for some time, so something must have occurred inside for him to come to me with such a heartfelt plea for forgiveness. I believed him. I believed him with all my heart. I took a deep breath, wanting desperately for him to be free from who he was. I didn't want to judge him by his past anymore. I didn't want to be afraid that the old Nate would surface again and spoil the peace.

I was grasping his hands tightly too. "I forgive you, Nate," I said, and I meant it. "I want you to be free. I want you to be a Christian—the man God wants you to be."

We hugged each other tightly, and I cried tears of release. Hope stirred inside me—something I hadn't felt in a very, very long time.

I called T. Hayes to see if he knew what had happened to bring about such an earnest conversation. He didn't know what happened, but he confirmed that Nate was a changed man. He was communicating differently with everyone. He just wasn't the same guy. I began thanking God every day for Nate. I couldn't believe that things were finally good between us—permanently good.

One day, I asked Nate for a new wedding ring. I didn't want any memory of how bad things had been. I wanted to forget it all and start fresh. Nate was very happy to do this, and he bought a beautiful, expensive ring. I cried tears of joy, letting all the bad memories of physical abuse, other women, alcohol, and bad times fade away.

In July, Nate came to me and said, "Dot, you always told me you wanted to have two children. I don't blame you if you don't ever want to have another child, but what do you think? What do you think about having another baby?"

I couldn't help but laugh. I knew he had been working this out in his mind before he ever came to me. Nate always had things figured out before he brought them up. Tré had always wanted a brother or sister. He prayed and asked God about having one all the time. I had been taking birth control pills since Tré was born, so he had seen me take them regularly and naturally asked me what they were for. I did my best to explain, but in Tré's mind, I was taking "birth pills" so I could get pregnant and have a baby. Sometimes he would come in my room and ask me if I had taken my pill so he could get his baby brother.

Our marriage was strong. We spent time with other believers, and there hadn't been any trouble with affairs or late nights or abuse in a long, long time. When Nate came to me and asked if I was ready to have another baby, I didn't even question it. "Absolutely!" I told him. It seemed infinitely clear to me that this was the right thing to do.

I stopped taking birth control pills, which worried young Tré.

"Mommy," he would say, his little brow furrowed with concern, "if you don't take your pill, I'm not going to have a brother or sister. You've got to take your pill!"

Before long, I conceived, and when I shared the happy news, we all celebrated. We were excited about the prospect of a new baby. Nate was ecstatic. He immediately was on the radio telling everybody, "My wife is pregnant!"

During my first trimester, I was nauseous and tired every day. It took a great deal of energy to keep up with Tré, but no matter how I felt, I still made sure that everything Nate needed was taken care of. I couldn't wait each night until I was finally able to crawl into bed and pray for a little sleep.

When I was three months pregnant, I started getting phone calls from a girl who said she was having an affair with Nate. I didn't want to believe it. At first I just hung up on her, thinking she was making crank calls or maybe wanting money out of Nate. She continued to call, only now she was giving me details—intimate details. I listened in horror, realizing she must be in a relationship with Nate, and here I was, pregnant and ill.

When I confronted Nate, he blew up. He shoved me against the wall and grabbed my throat with both hands, squeezing until I was gasping for air. He cursed and shouted and threw things. It was a horrible nightmare. I couldn't believe it! *How could this be happening again?* I crumpled into a heap on the floor, sobbing. Every painful episode from the past rushed in like a flood, drowning my hope and reminding me I was a complete fool for ever trusting this man.

The calls from the woman continued, and Nate started staying out late and drinking. Whenever he was at home, he was sullen and irritable. I knew better than to say anything to him, but I was so disgusted, tired, and angry that sometimes I would blurt out something stupid like, "Who is she, Nathaniel?"—and this would provoke a night of violent anger.

When I was five months pregnant, Nate came stumbling in during the wee hours of the morning, demanding that I get up and make him something to eat. I was exhausted, too tired to move out of bed. Nate shoved me hard, making sure I was awake and couldn't ignore him. I had to get up early to get Tré ready for school and make the hour-long drive, and I didn't want to get out of bed. I sat up and told Nate I was too tired. He pushed me off the bed and onto the floor.

"Make me somethin' to eat!" he shouted. I was too tired to argue back. I got up in silence and went to the kitchen.

A few nights later, he came in late again and demanded that I fix a meal. This time I didn't answer and didn't open my eyes. I just lay there, clutching the covers, refusing to acknowledge him. This just frustrated him even more. I squeezed my eyes shut and started to pray out loud, which made him very angry. It was a bad night.

This pattern continued. Some nights, I would get up and cook just to keep the peace. Other nights, I was too irritable and started yelling back. In fact, I was beginning to yell at Nate all the time. I could barely stand the sight of him. I was furious that he waited until I was pregnant to have a relapse. And I was angry with myself for trusting him again. The abuse was back in full swing, and there were nights I thought I would literally die.

I was constantly worried about Tré and who would take care of him if I died. I didn't want to leave him alone with Nate.

I talked with Ingrid about it, and she swore she would make sure Tré was taken care of if anything ever happened to me.

Tré was old enough to understand what was going on now. It broke my heart that he could hear us fighting. It scared me that he saw Nate shove me or choke me. I felt like a complete failure and just wanted to escape this horrible situation.

One night, I told Nate I was leaving him. I just couldn't live through this again. Whatever change he had made was totally erased, and I didn't have the strength to live with him anymore. This made him furious. He told me if I tried to leave him, he would kill me. The look in his eyes was so severe. The hatred and disdain were palpable. I believed him. I believed he would kill me if I tried to go. I was frightened. It felt like ice water was running through my veins.

I was desperate now. I cried out to God and prayed for protection and strength. I prayed for a way of escape. I asked God to protect Tré and help him to forget the horrible things he'd heard and seen. I meditated on Scripture as if my life depended on it. My prayers from Psalm 23 went something like this:

"The Lord is my shepherd; I shall not want."

God, I do want. I want to be free. I want to be safe. I am your child. You promised to protect me.

"He maketh me to lie down in green pastures: he leadeth me beside the still waters."

Yes, Lord. Please take me to green pastures. Please bring me to still, peaceful waters.

"He restoreth my soul."

My soul is weary, God. My spirit is alive and filled with you, but my flesh is totally spent, and my soul cries out in despair. Deliver me, God. Restore my soul.

"He leadeth me in the paths of righteousness for his name's sake."

God, I need you to show me the path. I know there is a path of righteousness for me even in this situation. Lead me there. I'll go.

"Yea, though I walk through the valley of the shadow of death, I will fear no evil."

But I am afraid. I am so afraid of this evil. I feel as though I am right in the center of death's dark, shadowed valley. How do I walk through it?

"For thou art with me; thy rod and thy staff they comfort me."

Yes. You are with me. When Nate hits me, he's hitting you. You are with me every moment, with every breath. You see it all. You hear it all. You care for me. You comfort me. You must have a plan for me.

"Thou preparest a table before me in the presence of mine enemies."

Is Nate my enemy, Lord? Or is Nate tormented and controlled by my real enemy? Your table is my provision, even when I am in captivity and surrounded by betrayal, lies, deceit, violence, anger, and abuse. Your table is my protection, keeping me safe, keeping me alive so I can care for Tré and protect my unborn child.

"Thou anointest my head with oil."

God, I need your healing. My mind needs to be healed. It is broken and bruised and weary and sad. Please let your oil of gladness flow over me. Let your healing balm flow. Anoint my head, Lord Jesus; anoint my head.

"My cup runneth over."

Yes, you have given me much to be thankful for. My cup runneth over with love for Tré and the baby who is not yet even born. My cup runneth over with the goodness of friends who care for me. My cup runneth over with your love. God, I love you. God, how I need you.

"Surely goodness and mercy shall follow me all the days of my life."

Your goodness overwhelms me. Your mercy is never-ending. Help

*me to understand. Help me to see, Lord. Let me feel your goodness
and mercy, and grant many days to my life.*

"And I will dwell in the house of the LORD for ever."

*Yes, Lord. I will dwell with you forever and ever. I will never leave
you. I will never forsake you. I will always call on your name. You
are my hiding place. You are my shield and my deliverer. You are my
song. You are my strong tower. You are my refuge.*

I meditated on this passage daily and took strength from its
words. I poured out my heart to God and gave him all my sorrow and grief, doubt and fear. I fellowshipped with God in my
suffering, and I found comfort in his presence and in his care.

I never once blamed God for what I was going through.
I never once felt like he wasn't protecting me. I felt like I had
placed myself in this situation. Over and over again, I had
made bad choices, and the consequences were pain, suffering,
and abuse.

Each day, I asked for God's protection over my life, over Tré,
and over our baby. My energy was totally spent. I knew if my
situation was going to change, it would absolutely take God's
intervention.

CHAPTER 21

The Last Straw

It is devastating to be abused by someone that
you love and think loves you in return.

U.S. Senator Dianne Feinstein

Nate had not come home for several nights. He was not at home as I stood over Tré's bed and watched him sleep. He was so peaceful, lying there with his little hands cupped under his cheek. *Such a handsome boy*, I thought to myself. Love for him welled up inside of me, and I reached down to stroke his head. Just then, the baby kicked me, as if he was jealous of the attention I was giving his brother. I patted my stomach and admonished him, "Stop that, now. I love you too, little one. Don't you ever think Mama doesn't love you with all her heart."

Tré rolled over, and his brow furrowed. A moment before, he had been totally peaceful, but now his face looked troubled, and he was restless, as if he was having a bad dream. I knelt down beside him, remembering how many bad dreams I had known in my childhood. I knew what it was like to be afraid for your mother. I knew what it was like to wish your daddy would stop yelling, stop hurting her ...

I ached inside. I never wanted my children to know the fear I felt as a child. I never wanted their dreams to become nightmares. I crawled into Tré's bed and held him close, tears streaming down my face.

"God," I prayed, "watch over my children and protect them from harm. Let them learn to love you with all their heart, soul, mind, and strength. Show me a way of escape. Keep me from the bondage of unforgiveness. I belong to you, Lord. Nate belongs to you. This isn't right. This isn't your plan for us. Guide me now. I don't know what to do. I need you ..."

I lay there, praying off and on throughout the night, stroking my stomach with one hand and cuddling Tré with the other. Remarkably, the night passed in peace. There was no argument with Nate, no demands—just God's peace, a respite from the storm. I didn't know how, but I knew God was going to take care of us. I knew this suffering would not last forever.

I was concerned for Tré. I knew all too well what he was going through. I knew the deep fear and anxiety that came from watching someone you love be battered and abused. No child should have to feel like they are on guard, waiting for something bad to happen, never knowing what will trigger the abuse, never quite feeling safe. I wanted him to know that prayer had the power to change things. I wanted him to know that kneeling at the feet of Jesus would always give him the strength and power to do whatever needed to be done.

On our long commute to school each morning, I prayed with Tré. I talked to him and tried to give him a safe place to vent what he was feeling. He was free to talk about anything and everything. I was strong for him. I did my best to explain things and share how God protected me and watched over us. I sometimes felt guilty that I had put him in a position to experience this pain, but I was so proud of how he handled things and how open he remained with me. We developed clear communication, and a lasting trust was established. During this season, our relationship grew strong and deep.

I was still working for Nate, arranging appearances and doing other things. As his popularity increased, I needed to work more closely with Valerie, his publicist. She was a nice, sweet Christian lady, and I enjoyed working with her. We talked often about coordinating Nate's calendar and keeping the schedule straight. In a moment when I was vulnerable, I confided in her that things were bad at home. She was kind and understanding and tried to reassure me that it didn't have to be that way. She thought it might help if she mentioned it to someone inside the Cowboys organization. She was sure they would intervene and make sure Nate got the help he needed and that I would be protected. Suddenly, I was frightened that I had told her. What if it got back to Nate? I told her she could tell no one. She might think it was going to help me, but it would only make things worse. Oh, how I regretted telling her. I hadn't intended to; it just sort of came out. I wasn't myself these days — tired, bruised, swollen — and being pregnant didn't help.

It had been a bad night. Nate had come home very late, and the abuse was worse than usual. I dropped Tré off at school and sat in my car for a moment, wondering about what to do next. When Nate first woke up, he was not usually violent. In fact, even if we had been through a bad night, he often didn't seem to remember what had happened. I was never quite sure what to expect. I was exhausted beyond belief, and my body was sore all over — like one giant bruise, so I put the car in gear and headed for home. Nate was still sleeping, so I went into Tré's room to lie down. I set an alarm just in case I fell asleep, wanting to be sure I had enough time to shower and dress before I left again to pick up Tré from school.

I felt better when I woke up, and the sun was shining as I pulled out of the driveway and headed for Fort Worth Christian. *Why do I put up with this?* I asked myself. *Why don't I just leave him? It isn't my fault that Nate beats me. It isn't my fault that he sleeps with other women. I don't deserve this. Tré doesn't deserve this. I can't bring another baby into this horrible situation. I can't!*

Just then my cell phone rang, and it startled me. It was Nate. I stared at it, frightened that Nate knew what I was thinking. I swallowed hard and answered.

"Where you at?" Nate asked.

"I'm on my way to pick up Tré," I replied. He was silent.

"Nate," I said, "why are you treating me this way? Why are you doing all this?"

I felt as if something had uncorked inside of me. "I can't do this anymore. I *won't* do this anymore. I'm leaving you. Don't worry; I'm not gonna run to the media or anything. I won't tell a soul what has happened, but I have to go. I just have to go." Silence.

"Nate," I said firmly, though my whole body was shaking, "I want a divorce."

Nate was furious and started shouting. I couldn't believe I had told him what I was thinking. It's a good thing the route was so familiar, because I know I wasn't paying attention to the road — it was like the car was driving itself.

Nate ranted for a few minutes and then told me we would talk when I got home — and I had better come home. Then he asked, "Who did you go tellin' my business to?"

I froze. *Oh, God*, I thought, *did Valerie . . . ?*

"Don't make me come and find you," Nate snarled. "If I have to come find you, I'll kill you." He hung up.

I picked up Tré and thought about just driving away, but I was too afraid. I knew Nate would never lay a hand on Tré — at least I didn't think he would — but I was certain I was in for a very rough night. I knew if I didn't go home, he would find me.

I called Valerie. "Did you tell anybody?" I asked. "Who did you tell?"

Valerie was stunned and very upset. She felt like someone needed to reach out and help me. She meant to help. She didn't realize how desperate my situation was.

Without thinking, I drove to Ingrid's house. She would know what to do. I arrived a total mess. We sent the boys to another room to play, and I wrote a letter stating that if I turned up dead, it was because Nate had killed me. I made her promise not to read it, but if anything happened to me, she had to take it to the police. She promised, and I watched her put the letter in her safe. I was scared I was going to die, and I was even more afraid of what would happen to Tré if I did.

"Ingrid," I said, "you must promise me that if anything ever happens to me, you will raise Tré. I don't want him to grow up with Nate if I'm not there."

I was worried that since Ingrid had never told Monte about my situation, he might not agree to take Tré from Nate. I knew how charming Nate was to everybody else, and I could see him telling Monte I had gone crazy or something, and I was sure Nate would get his way. Ingrid promised me she would raise Tré, and I asked her to put that commitment in writing, sign it, and give me a copy. Then I watched her as she put her copy in the safe. I let out a sigh of relief. Tré would be taken care of.

Ingrid didn't cry, but her countenance betrayed her sadness. I knew she was scared for me. I sat in her home, thinking that if my family knew what I was going through, they would risk everything to protect me, but they didn't know. I thought about my aunt in Virginia; I knew she would help me, but she didn't know either. Sheila, Bug—many names came to mind, but no one knew I was in danger. I hadn't told anyone, and now it was too late. Nate was going to kill me; I was sure of it.

"You promise me you will take Tré?" I asked Ingrid again.

"Yes, yes, of course I will," Ingrid said, her eyes completely sincere and her face filled with concern.

"You should not go back there," she said. "Stay here. Don't go home."

"I have to," I said. "I have to go back. You don't understand."

"You don't understand," I repeated. "I have to reassure him that I haven't gone to the police. He told me I have to bring Tré home. I have to go."

I collected Tré and tried to prepare him as we drove home.

"Tré," I said.

"Yes, Mama?"

"When we get home, I want you to stay in the car until I come back outside to get you, okay?"

"Why?" he asked.

"Listen, baby, I'm going to turn on some music for you. You just put your little headphones on and pretend like you're driving the car. Can you do that? Your daddy is really upset about some things, and I don't want you to come inside until he calms down."

"Okay," he said. It was like any other day to Tré. He was used to Daddy being angry and Mommy getting hurt. He had learned to hide and be quiet and wait until the storms blew over. It was sad.

We were almost home. An icy calm settled over me. I expected the worst. I didn't even mind — except that I cared so much about Tré. If Nate killed me, I would be with Jesus and free from suffering. *If only Tré* — I couldn't think about it or I would break down and cry. I felt the baby kick, and I was sorry I would never get to hold him in my arms.

I put the car in park and took the keys out of the ignition. I got out Tré's music and his headphones and told him to wait for me in the car — he was *not* to come inside. I looked at him, hugged him hard, and kissed the top of his head.

Slowly I walked through the front door, not knowing what to expect. *Would he beat me? Would he shoot me?* I didn't even think we had a gun in the house, but there was one in the guesthouse. I walked into the kitchen, shaking. I didn't know what to expect this time, but I knew this was different from anything I'd been through before. Nate was there waiting.

"What the f____ are you doing?" he shouted.

"What do you mean?" I answered.

"You know what I mean. If you *ever* tell *anyone* my business *ever* again, I'll kill you."

I sat down at the dining room table, preparing for a rant. "I'm tired of this, Nate. I want to be free from you. Can't you just let me be free from you? Free to go on?"

"The only freedom you're ever gonna get is if I kill you!" he said. Then I saw the gun lying on the counter. It was the rifle he used to shoot snakes when he was out with the dogs. I stared at the gun. Nate followed my gaze, and his lips curled into a snarl. He wanted me to be afraid.

He started shouting again and moved toward the table. The tabletop was made from heavy, beveled glass. I was sitting at the end of it in front of the large picture window in the dining room. Nate grabbed the edge of the table and shoved it toward me. Pure instinct made me scoot back in the chair as fast as I could, fearing the table would plunge into my abdomen and hurt the baby. The table just grazed my stomach as I scrambled out of the way. It came crashing to the floor, somehow not shattering but breaking the granite tile as it struck with a heavy thud.

I stared at the table in disbelief. He could have hurt the baby. Explosive anger welled up inside of me. Adrenaline rushed through my body, and hot, angry words came to the surface.

"You're sick!" I shouted at him, looking at the mess on the floor. "You are sick, Nathaniel Newton! What is wrong with you?"

Nate glared at me and started walking toward the counter, toward the gun.

"Enough is enough," I screamed. "I'm going to the police.

We have a child together, Nathaniel. We have another child on the way. Do you want to hurt the baby? What do you think you're doing? I'm going to the authorities—do you hear me? I'm calling the police!"

I was still sitting in the dining room chair where I had scooted to avoid being hit by the table when, quick as a flash, Nate had the gun in his hands and pointed it straight at me. I froze.

"What are you doing?" I asked, shaking.

"I'm going to kill you, that's what," Nate said, leveling the gun right between my eyes.

I held my breath, waiting for him to pull the trigger. *Oh, God*, I prayed silently, *don't let Tré find me here like this.*

Nate kept the gun pointed at my face. I don't know how long he stood there, but neither one of us said a word. I was shaking all over, tears streaming down my face. I could hear my heart pounding in my ears, and I felt like I was going to faint. I wanted to run, but my feet were glued to the floor—I couldn't move.

Nate kept the barrel pointed steady between my eyes, then he moved the barrel a few inches to the right and pulled the trigger, smashing a bullet through the window behind me, shattering it into a million pieces.

I screamed and fell to the floor, grabbing my ears.

"Nate!" I screamed.

"You won't call the police; I'll kill you first," he said and rushed out the door, jumped in his vehicle, and sped off.

I don't know how long I knelt on the floor, but I suddenly panicked, wondering where Tré was. *Did Nate take Tré?*

I went outside and Tré was not in the car. *Where was he?* I ran back in the house. *Did he see anything?*

"Tré, come here!" I shouted.

Tré came running toward me, and I scooped him up and

held him tightly. There was a gaping hole where the window should have been and glass was shattered all over the place. We got in the car and drove away.

I called T. Hayes and told him what had happened.

"Are you okay? Are you hurt?" he asked, concern thick in his voice.

"I'm fine," I said, convincing no one.

"Don't stay there right now," he said. "Why don't you come here for a while?"

Dutifully, I obeyed. I didn't have the energy to make any decisions on my own. His wife, Lisa, was also expecting a baby, and I knew if I went there, I would be safe. Sooner or later, I knew Nate would call T. Hayes—he always did.

Tré was quiet in the car beside me. I didn't think he'd seen anything, but he must have heard the shot. He didn't say a word, and I didn't trust myself to speak to him about it.

I called Randy, our builder, and said as nonchalantly as I could, "Randy, can you go over to the house and take care of something for me?"

"Sure," he said. "What's up?"

"There's some shattered glass at the house"—I took a deep breath—"in the kitchen . . ." My voice broke.

"You okay?" he asked.

"Uh-huh," I managed to croak out. "Thanks, Randy." I hung up and drove to T. Hayes's house. The next day, Randy called. "Are you okay, Dorothy?" he asked.

"I'm fine," I said.

"I found shotgun shells on the floor," he said. "Are you sure you're okay?"

"I'm fine," I said again. "Are you at my house now?"

"Yes, I'm just finishing up. I've taken care of everything good as new."

"Is Nate there?" I asked.

"No, ma'am, he isn't," Randy replied. "Do you need something?"

"No … no, I'm just fine, Randy," I said. "Thanks for everything."

I didn't want to go back to the house until T. Hayes had heard from Nate. He would know when it was safe.

I took Tré to school the next day and called T. Hayes before driving back to the house. The window was fixed like nothing had ever happened. There were two shotgun shells sitting on the counter. Randy had set the table back on its feet, and the only visible evidence of the trauma was a chip in the granite floor where the table had fallen and another chip in the beveled tabletop edge that had struck the floor.

An uneasiness was in the air, thick and foreboding. I thanked God I was alive, and I asked for his guidance. I knew I couldn't stay with Nate anymore. From T. Hayes, I gathered that Nate had cleared out, so I knew I had a little time to think and figure things out.

I looked around my house — our house. We had known happiness here. It hadn't been too long ago that things were good between us. I thought about Nate's excitement when I announced my pregnancy, and the tears came pouring out — silent tears that no one but God saw or heard.

CHAPTER 22

Humiliation

I see grace groweth best in the winter.

Samuel Rutherford

It was three weeks before I saw Nate again. He turned up to tell me he was going to Florida to train with a bicyclist to get in shape before training camp began. I didn't care. I was glad he would be gone so I could figure out what to do. I didn't have any money of my own and didn't have access to any of Nate's money—I didn't even know how much he had.

When I found out he was seeing another woman in Florida, the news didn't shock me. The woman who had been calling me to tell me about her affair with Nate started calling again, but now she was different; she was angry with Nate. I don't know why I did it, but I contacted Nate in Florida and told him, "I think you're about to have legal problems with this girl." A week later, Nate came home and apologized to me for his behavior. He wanted to work things out between us.

"No," I told him, emotionless, "I really just want you out of my life. The sooner you go to training camp, the better; that way I don't have to see you."

Nate apologized again. "We can work this out . . ." he began.

"No, Nathaniel, we can't," I said. "I'm leaving you. I don't care if you kill me. I have it worked out so Tré will be taken care of. I am prepared to die. If you hurt me again, I will go to the authorities and get help. I've already spoken with an attorney, and you are going to be served with divorce papers. You can take whatever you want. I don't want anything from you; I just want out. You can kill me if you want to, but I have already told the attorney that you plan to do that, so go right ahead; the police will know it was premeditated."

Nate was enraged. He pushed me up against the wall and struck me. I crumpled to the floor to protect my stomach, and Nate kicked me.

"I'm having to deal with enough right now, b____!" he shouted. "I can't be bothered with you too, do you hear me? This girl is trying to threaten me. I need you now, Dot. Just when I need you, you think you're gonna leave? You're not gonna be there? You gonna walk away from me like everybody else?"

I packed some things for Tré and left. I headed to Louisiana. Nate didn't try to stop me. Obviously, I hadn't called the police or the media, so I guess he figured I wouldn't say anything to my family either. He was used to me keeping my mouth shut and remaining the dutiful wife. I always came back.

I contemplated telling my family. While I was driving to see them, I rehearsed my story. When I actually got there, I couldn't go through with it. I don't know why; I just couldn't do it. Everyone kept asking about Nate and wondering how he was doing — they all loved him. Why wouldn't they? He had always been so nice to them. They had no idea he was a different person behind closed doors. I couldn't seem to make myself tell them I was in trouble, even though I desperately wanted their help.

While there, Tré became ill. He got so sick that I had to take him to a hospital in New Orleans. We were there all day, and when he was discharged, I took him to my mother's place in Buras, sixty miles away. Nate called, and I told him about Tré. He told me the woman was filing a lawsuit against him, accusing him of rape. He begged me to come home, telling me how much he needed me. He promised me that if I would come home and see him through the trial, he would give me a divorce.

I wanted that divorce. I was paying an attorney $250 per hour, and I didn't know where I was going to find the money if Nate contested. Holding out the divorce was the right bait for me. I wanted it, and if Nate was willing to set me free, then I would go home and deal with whatever I had to in order to buy my freedom.

The woman accused Nate of sexual assault, and it made the national news. I was humiliated. I went back home, and Nate disappeared to escape the media frenzy. I don't know where he went, but he wasn't around, and I didn't care. I was growing closer to term, and my focus was on taking care of Tré and the baby.

I hardly heard from Nate during the last few weeks of my pregnancy. I was so sick that it seemed like all of my energy was expended going back and forth to the doctor. I was scheduled to be induced on July 15. Nate called the weekend before and asked about when I thought I might go into labor. I had no idea whether or not he would show up — it didn't matter to me. I wanted Ingrid to be with me in the delivery room. She was a steady, constant, and loving force in my life, and I wanted her by my side. When I was with her, my heart was lighter and my troubles melted away, and I felt strong and free. I wanted my mother too. I needed her support. I arranged for her to come to stay with me so she and Ingrid could be in the delivery room and be around to help out with Tré.

I went to the hospital for my appointment, and Nate showed up. I was so disappointed. *Why had he come?* I couldn't deny his rights as the father, so he came into the delivery room with me, and Ingrid and my mom waited outside. The delivery room is still a blur to me, but when it was all over, I had a healthy baby boy weighing in at ten pounds, two and a half ounces. The same feelings of awe, wonder, and unconditional love washed over me, just as they had when Tré was born. When I held my little boy, everything else receded. Nothing else was as important as taking care of this little one and loving him with all my heart.

I still didn't have a name for him, and I had promised Tré he could name the baby, since he had prayed for one with such unwavering faith. When Tré saw his brother in the hospital nursery, without even thinking he said, "I know what we can name him."

"What?" I asked, chuckling at his enthusiasm.

"We can name him King 'cause he looks like he's the king of the nursery!"

"King it is!" I said, laughing. I had no qualms with the name King because the greatest king I knew was the King of kings — Jesus Christ, the Son of the living God. Tré's excitement could not be contained. He was overjoyed to have a brother of his very own. He was so proud that his brother was bigger than all the other babies. He couldn't wait to hold him and wanted to know when we could take him home. Tré named him King, but Nate also wanted the baby to have his name, so we settled on Nate King Newton for this special baby boy. I celebrated his arrival with true joy. Baby King was a gift from God — this was undeniable.

I was released from the hospital and went home. Nate went off to training camp, so there was peace while I recovered from the delivery. When King was just six weeks old, Nate came home from training camp for a court appearance regarding the accusation of sexual assault. I received a subpoena to appear as a witness. Because I had received so many calls from this woman in which she gave details about their trips together and how he took care of her and her child, my testimony was needed to prove they were in a consensual relationship. The woman had been harassing me with phone calls from the time

I was three months pregnant with King. I was humiliated and upset that I had to leave King and go to the courthouse to testify on Nate's behalf.

I arrived at the scheduled time and stood outside the courtroom, waiting for my turn to go in. Nate stood outside with his attorney, but neither of them engaged me in any conversation. Never once had I been given any details about the trial or about Nate's part in the relationship with the woman. I never asked about anything, and Nate never volunteered anything. I felt hollow inside — no emotion, just numb. I didn't really care what happened to Nate. I didn't believe he had raped the woman, but I honestly could not manage to find any warm or concerned feelings for him. I was filled with disgust, and I wanted nothing to do with him.

I was called not into the courtroom but into a private room with the jury. I was told to tell exactly what it was I had been experiencing with the plaintiff, and I gave all the information as it had happened. I also told the people in the room that Nate and I were experiencing serious marital problems, but I believed God would fight that battle for me. I told them it was important for me to be able to separate those things and focus on the facts at hand. I asked them to concentrate on the facts relevant to the case and not on Nate's status as a cheating husband. I told them I did not believe this was a case of rape but that this relationship had been consensual. I told them I was upset — very upset — but the truth is what it is: I did not believe Nate had raped this woman.

When I came out of the room, I was completely convinced Nate would not be convicted.

"What happened in there?" Nate asked.

"Don't worry," I said. "You'll be free as usual."

Nate and his attorney finally had a conversation with me,

a detailed conversation that made me sick to my stomach. I was shocked when I learned the details of what had really happened. I shouldn't have been shocked after everything I had been through with Nate, but I was shocked nevertheless. In fact, I was speechless. I stared at Nate like he was a total stranger. I wanted him to stay away from me forever. I wanted to leave that courthouse and have it all be over.

I drove to Ingrid's house to pick up six-week-old King. She asked me to come inside, and I sat down in a chair, wanting to cry, but I couldn't. My tears had dried up. I had no feelings whatsoever. Inside, I was crumbling, but on the outside, my tears wouldn't flow.

Ingrid and her mother were in the room with me, but I was unable to speak. I couldn't tell them anything. They didn't know what to say to me, and I couldn't find any words to say to them. I just kept thinking to myself, *I can't believe my baby is six weeks old — Nate's baby — and I'm in the courthouse to defend him over sleeping with another woman. I can't believe it.*

Just as I predicted, Nate was not convicted. *We've been through so much in the last six months*, I thought to myself. *Surely nothing else will happen.* Things were calm. Nate kept his distance from me, I suppose with the idea that he'd give me time to get over the fact that I had to testify on his behalf against his lover. I used the calmness to approach Nate.

"I think it's best if we just go our separate ways," I said. "I need to be free of this marriage — it isn't really much of a marriage anyway. I'll take care of the boys. If you'll just help me out with three months' rent, I'll be able to get a job by then and won't need anything else from you. You owe me that much, Nate," I said.

"Dot, just wait awhile. Just a little while. Can you just wait a little while? Everything is going to be better," he replied.

I let out a deep, heavy sigh. I knew he wasn't going to give me a divorce. I knew he wasn't going to give me money for rent or child care. *How can I find a job and move away from him without some help?* I thought. I felt totally trapped and completely powerless to change my situation.

From that day on, I prayed more than ever before. I asked God to help me change things in my life. I trusted no one. I had lived my entire life afraid. I had placed Nate's needs, Nate's career, Nate's wants, ahead of everything else. Something inside of me was so twisted and broken that I thought more about Nate than about my own safety. I felt like I had done something to deserve the abuse — like I had to pay for my past sins. I was too afraid to go to the police. I knew if I did, Nate would worm his way out of any trouble, like he always did. The rules were different for him. He was a celebrity. I thought about all the trouble he had caused and how he always seemed to escape suffering any real consequences from his actions. Every time — not guilty, not convicted. I felt like every effort on my part was completely futile.

I lived a lie, a double life. I played my role as a devoted, faithful wife so well in public that no one ever suspected a thing. No one knew I was miserable, broken, and bruised, crying out for deliverance and desperate to escape. Ingrid and T. Hayes had some idea, but even what they knew was limited and filtered. To my friends and the world around me, I lived a dream life. I was married to a celebrity, a professional athlete. Nate was the life of the party, showering everyone with gifts, giving them what they wanted, and treating them well. We had a nice home. We had nice cars. People assumed I had a lot of money. I knew it wouldn't make sense to any of my friends if I went to them to ask for financial help. I thought of going to Ingrid, and I know she would gladly have helped, but how could she give me money without telling Monte what it was for? I didn't want him to know. *You're on your own*, I said to myself. *Just you and God.*

Why didn't I tell my family? Surely if I had made my situation known, they would have intervened. I was too frightened to take the chance. Nate had threatened to kill me if I told anyone his business, and the image of him pointing that gun at my head was as fresh in my memory as the day it happened.

Growing up, I promised myself I would never get in the same situation my mother was in—unable to escape because she was financially dependent on my abusive stepfather. Here I was, repeating history. I took the bad with the good and prayed for a way out.

CHAPTER 23

My Shield

God is my defender. My God loves me,
and he goes in front of me.

Psalm 59:9–10 NCV

I lived my life going through the motions. The cycle of abuse (verbal, physical, sexual) rotated with cycles of calm — Nate keeping his distance, Nate promising to change, Nate going through some self-inflicted trauma. I found a way to separate myself into two people. I was one way with Nate. Whatever he asked or demanded from me, I found some way to comply. Sometimes I yelled back and said horrible things; sometimes I struggled against him; and sometimes I just gave in like a wounded dog, but I did what I had to do to survive.

The other me lived a totally different life. When I left the house, I tucked away that abused, weary, broken Dorothy and put on the strong, tender, kindhearted Dorothy who cared deeply about other people's pain and reached out in any way I could. When I spent time with Ingrid, I was a different person. When I spent time with people, I was a different person. When I spent time alone with God, he strengthened me and filled me and taught me things about my own character and my own faults. He spoke to me about my hatred and the bondage I was in.

"Lord," I prayed, "please keep me safe from all danger and harm. Help me to have a better attitude and plenty of gratitude. Clear my mind so I can truly hear from you. Broaden my mind so I can accept what you are saying to me. Help me not to whine about the things I have no control over. Renew my mind so I won't feel guilty about all the bad choices I've made that led me here. I know that even when I cannot pray, you listen to my heart, so remove the hatred that is lurking there. Please cleanse me from it."

I kept praying. "My struggles, trials, and tribulations are beyond belief right now, and only you really know what they are. God, help me through them so I can be a blessing to others someday. Keep me strong so I will not give up, Lord. Keep me uplifted so I may have words of encouragement for others, even during this time."

And earnestly, passionately, I continued. "God, I feel like I'm lost right now. I'm in the wilderness, and I haven't been able to find my way in a long, long time. I need your guidance. I believe you can change people and you can change things. Bring a change in my life — bring it quickly; please hasten. I am your child. I do not have the strength to take any more, to carry this burden one moment longer. I need you. I need you now."

I repeated this prayer over and over, and it gave me peace. I meditated on the New Testament story of Paul and Silas in prison, their backs badly beaten and their feet shackled — and yet they sang praises to God and worshiped him, even in the middle of their horrible, seemingly hopeless situation. They sang praises to God even when they were powerless to set themselves free. This was me! I could sing praises to God in the midst of my situation, and his peace came upon me and surpassed all my understanding. Somehow I knew I would be okay.

I began to spend more time asking for forgiveness and less time pleading for mercy. I started listening more and talking less. I learned how to be still. Tentatively, I began trusting God. Ingrid and I continued studying the Bible together and also attended Bible studies during the day while the kids were in school. This kept me encouraged — it kept me alive.

God spoke to my heart. He had been speaking all along,

but I was finally still enough to hear his voice. God's goodness penetrated my heart and my spirit, and change took root inside of me. Nate's antics no longer had the same effect. It was like I lived inside a bubble of God's peace. I filtered every word that came out of my mouth and every move I made through God's Word.

When I thought about not being able to make it on my own while supporting two kids, when I was filled with regret over giving up my career to support Nate, I quoted this promise from Scripture: "My God shall supply all your need according to his riches in glory by Christ Jesus" (Philippians 4:19).When I felt too weary to go on, I relied on the words of Christ: "Come unto me, all ye that labour and are heavy laden, and I will give you rest. Take my yoke upon you, and learn of me; for I am meek and lowly in heart: and ye shall find rest unto your souls. For my yoke is easy, and my burden is light" (Matthew 11:28–30). I committed Scripture to memory, inscribing it on the tablets of my heart. It was my weapon. It was my shield.

I prayed diligently for Tré. He was, for the most part, a happy-go-lucky child. He was very smart and very protective of me and King. Still, there was too much heaviness on a boy so young. He had seen too much. He had heard things no little boy should ever have to hear, and I was worried about what kind of man he would grow up to be. *Would he solve his problems by lashing out in selfish anger? Was history doomed to repeat itself?* I prayed it would not. I spoke words of life over him. I prayed over him and declared good things over his future. I declared that he and King would grow up to love God with all their heart, soul, mind, and strength and not repeat my mistakes, not repeat Nate's mistakes. I loved these little boys with a fierce, protective love. They filled my life with purpose and gave me a mission greater than mere survival.

CHAPTER 24

Divorce

If the numbers we see in domestic
violence were applied to terrorism or gang
violence, the entire country would be
up in arms, and it would be the lead
story on the news every night.

U.S. Congressman Mark Green

The 1997 season began, and Nate and I were in a season of calm. It was almost as if we were living separately under the same roof. I never asked him about the details of anything going on with his life outside our home, but things were not good. He was getting into trouble more frequently—DUIs, car accidents, and he even faced a misdemeanor for disorderly conduct after a loud argument with a fan who wanted his autograph. I kept my distance from these things and did my best not to get involved.

I took advantage of the season of calm to approach Nate about the divorce. "I think it's best if we go our separate ways," I said. "I need to be free from the marriage. We can each just go our own path. I'll take care of the boys. You can keep all the money; just help me out with three months' rent while I get a job."

"Dot, just wait a while. Just wait a little while. Everything is going to be better," was Nate's answer. I knew he didn't want me to leave. I knew he wouldn't give me a divorce. I knew that in his own twisted way he loved me, but I wanted out. I didn't want to live a double life anymore.

The Cowboys had a "White House" scandal at some point during all of this. There was a house (they called it The White House) located near the team's Valley Ranch practice facility where some of the players brought women for sex and had frequent parties. When questioned about this by the *Star-Telegram*, Nate removed all doubt about his involvement: "We got a little place over here where we're running whores in and out, trying to be responsible, and we're criticized for that too." I was disgusted.

My humiliation seemed to have no end. I was constantly embarrassed by Nate's public behavior, but I stood by him, no matter what. It seemed like every time I approached him about leaving, he got into some crisis again and needed me.

We continued to have seasons of relative calm followed by seasons of violence in which he would be verbally abusive, push me, and grab me by the throat. I never knew exactly what to expect.

I drew closer and closer to God for my strength. It seemed like the worse things got for me physically and emotionally, the more my spirit soared. I was filled with the Holy Spirit, and he was indeed my Comforter. No matter how bad things were with Nate, my soul was at peace with God. Nate had no control there. He couldn't spoil it. He couldn't interrupt it. He couldn't harm it.

Nate knew I was close to God. When it came to this area of my life, Nate still had me on a pedestal. There was almost a reverence from him about it—he never wanted to mess with that. He counted on the fact that I prayed, and on rare occasions he still asked me to pray for him, though he wasn't willing to pray on his own. In his mind, God was reserved for "good" people who already had their act together.

Nate was involved in another affair. In the past, he was careful to protect me from knowing about them, but he had grown careless. Not only was he coming home in the wee hours of the morning; he was leaving evidence all around— condoms, notes, receipts. I knew he was unfaithful and had probably been so for our entire life together. When he wanted sex, I was frightened. *What if he gives me a disease?* I began collecting the evidence, wanting to have proof of his indiscretions so I would at last be able to leave, even if he wasn't willing to consent to a divorce.

In the summer of 1998, just before Nate went to training camp, I found evidence of yet another relationship. I became enraged. Nate came into the house, and I lost all my fear of him. I screamed at him. I accused him. I was crying and shouting and storming around the room. It took Nate completely off guard—he wasn't used to this kind of behavior from me. He grabbed me by my arms to bring me under control.

"F_____ you!" I screamed.

It was like I had thrown ice water on him. He was so startled. I never used that kind of language, and it shocked him.

"Dot," he said, his face contorted, "what's wrong with you? That's not like you. Calm down, now. Calm down."

"That's right," I said through clenched teeth, "I said it— f_____ you!"

Nate was mortified. He shook me. "Get hold of yourself, Dot! Settle down." He let me go, and I crumpled into a heap on the floor.

"Who am I?" I said, almost in a whisper. I was genuinely frightened at my own anger. This wasn't me.

Could I hurt him? I wondered. I shuddered. *Yes, I could.* In fact, I wanted to.

I shuddered again, trying to shake myself out of whatever it was that had taken hold of me. I went to my room, got on my face, and prayed. I knew I could never give in to that anger again. I rolled over, looking up to heaven, and prayed, "God, you've got to do something spectacular to get me out of this situation. I don't ever want to feel this way again. I never want to lose control like that again. Help me, Jesus. Help me now."

In 1999, Nate was cut from the Cowboys. It was a crushing blow to him. He worked hard to get a contract with the Carolina Panthers and then announced we were moving to North Carolina. My first thought was, *This is my way out.*

"No, Nate," I said. "I can't take the boys to North Carolina. Tré is involved in sports and has good teachers. Taking him out of school is not good for him. Think of Tré. We need to stay here."

Miraculously, I convinced Nate that I should stay behind in Texas with the boys while he moved to Carolina. My heart lifted. It felt as if God had stepped in and offered me a way of escape. I was rescued! I could use this time to find a job and get established. I knew this was the beginning of my breakthrough.

Tré attended school Monday through Friday and played football on Saturday, so we only went to North Carolina on holidays. We couldn't watch Nate play all his games—and I didn't want to. I was happy on my own with the boys.

Another American Express bill came to the house, and I saw charges for airline tickets to and from Carolina—yet another woman. I didn't care. At least I was safe. I was involved in Bible study and enjoying "normal" life. I felt lighthearted. If Nate needed another woman in Carolina so I could stay at home, so be it.

At Christmas, Nate demanded I come to see him and bring the boys with me. I couldn't think of any good reason why we couldn't go, so I packed them up and flew out to meet him. When I arrived and began unpacking, I came across pieces of women's jewelry. Right there in plain sight was proof Nate was seeing someone. I flew home the next day. I was glad to be away from him. I was happy he was living in North Carolina. He could stay there as long as he liked. In January, the season came to an end. I was dreading it, knowing it meant Nate would move back home with us. He had injured his shoulder, which was going to require surgery to repair it. It had not been a good season for Nate, and with the injury, his football career was in serious jeopardy. I had physical evidence of a long-term affair, and I was ready to go to an attorney. Nate asked me to stay with him during the surgery and his recovery. He promised that if I stayed, and if I agreed to use his attorney and accept his terms, then he would give me a divorce. I consented to everything. All I wanted was out.

"Fine," I said. "I'll stay until you are recovered. I'll use your attorney, and I don't care what the terms are as long as I get to leave." I meant every word I said.

February came, and we scheduled an appointment with Nate's attorney. The attorney told me we could split everything down the middle, and Nate would pay $2,000 a month in child support. "Down the middle?" I asked, shocked, "Down the middle—what does that look like?" I didn't need to be shocked; there wasn't anything left to split. Nate was out of money. He had managed to spend everything he'd earned over the years. All that remained was the house. We had paid cash for the house and owned it outright. The plan was for me to stay in the house with the boys until it sold and then we would split the proceeds—and that would be the end of that.

March was coming, and we had already booked and paid for a trip to Jamaica. Tré had learned about Jamaica in school and dreamed about going for a long time. The Martins' son Drew was flying in from Jacksonville to join us. I didn't know how to back out of the trip without letting Tré down, and I wasn't ready to tell the Martins about the divorce. They had been so good to Tré, treating him like one of their own, that I just didn't think I could cancel. I told Nate I would go on the trip, but we would not sleep together. I still wanted a divorce.

On the trip, Nate was very relaxed and attentive to the boys. It was actually the best trip we ever took together. I felt as if a giant weight had been lifted from my shoulders. I didn't want Nate out of the boys' lives completely. He was their father. He had never been abusive to them, so this arrangement was like an experiment for me.

When we returned from Jamaica, Nate disappeared. I had no idea where he went. I didn't hear from him again until June. It was time for us to appear in court, and the attorney told me that only one of us had to be present, so I didn't worry about trying to find Nate. I didn't have to worry though; he called.

"Dot, are you sure you want to do this?" he asked. "I mean really sure? I'm out of football now. I always promised you if you would wait until my career was over, I would be the best husband ever. You don't need to do this. There won't be any more football. It will be different now. Things are gonna be totally different now."

"No," I answered, feeling genuinely sad that things never worked out. "I'm sorry. I'm going before the judge tomorrow."

The next morning, I went to the courthouse. I had not cried in a very long time. In fact, I couldn't even remember the last time I'd cried. I didn't have time to cry and feel sorry for myself. But standing there before the judge, the tears flowed unchecked. When the judge asked me to state my name, no words came out of my mouth.

"Mrs. Newton," the judge said sternly, not an ounce of sympathy in his voice. "Mrs. Newton, you do need to speak up," he said, frowning. It sounded like Nate's voice, stern and cross. I shook myself, snapped out of it, and went through the rest of the proceeding without another tear.

I made arrangements to have dinner that night with Ingrid. I hadn't told anyone I was getting a divorce. I left my kids with a babysitter and pulled into Ingrid's driveway to pick her up. She slid into the passenger seat, smiling, ready for an outing.

"Ingrid," I said, "we're not going anywhere, okay? I need to be by myself right now." I paused, and Ingrid studied me, sensing something was wrong. "I'm divorced," I finally said.

"What?" she said, and then she repeated, "You're *what?*"

She was shocked. I had confided many things to Ingrid, but I hadn't told her everything. I suppose I wasn't sure if it was actually going to happen. Until I had actually signed the papers and knew it was for real, I hadn't wanted to tell her.

"Divorced," I said again, letting out a long, slow sigh. "I'm divorced, Ingrid. I need to make some calls to my family. Do you mind if we skip dinner?"

I called my mom, my biological dad, my aunt and uncle in Virginia, Lynn and K-Mart, T. Hayes, and several other people. In the days and weeks to come, I slowly began telling people what my life had been like. Shock was the common response. No one but Ingrid and T. Hayes knew anything about the abuse.

To the public, I was living the perfect life of a celebrity wife, so my divorce seemed to come out of the blue. The media reports of Nate's trouble with women, fighting, and drinking revealed an ugly thread through our public life, but I had stayed with him through all of it. No one knew how rough things had been for me, and I guess my decision seemed sudden or even rash.

As agreed, I kept living in the house. In July, I held a birthday party for King, and Nate showed up. He was pleasant and amiable — and then he disappeared again.

One night he called and wanted to know where we were, telling me he was in town and wanted to see the kids. I wouldn't tell him where I was, but I reassured him that I would make sure he could see the boys. We drove up to the house and saw

Nate's truck parked at the back where the guesthouse was. The boys were excited, bouncing up and down. "Daddy! Daddy!" they shouted. I drove around to the back so the boys could run and find him, and there he was—with a woman. I was furious. I got out of the car, picked up a rock, and threw it in his direction. "Get off the property," I shouted. "Just go. Get off the property!"

Nate rushed toward me and held me. "Calm down, Dot. Calm down. Don't worry; I'm gonna get her off the property."

"Don't you touch me, Nathaniel Newton. You will not hurt me again!" I pulled out my cell phone and called the police and then T. Hayes.

The officer came and was jovial with Nate. With me, he was firm and authoritative. "Mrs. Newton, I've been told his name is on the deed, same as yours. He has every right to be here. You need to calm down." I stared at him in shock. It was just as I imagined it would be if I ever found the nerve to call the police.

T. Hayes arrived, and I ran over to him. "Do you see how the officer is treating me? Look at him with Nate. He's over there laughing and talking about football. It's always like this when I need help!" Bad memories flooded my mind, and I fought to regain control.

Being divorced was supposed to keep this from happening again. Nate was supposed to be out of my life, unable to harass or threaten me any longer. Even my divorce was a disappointment.

PART 5

Moving On

CHAPTER 25

Working Things Out

Disappointment to a noble soul is
what cold water is to burning metal;
it strengthens, tempers, intensifies,
but never destroys it.

Eliza Tabor

In 2001, I rented an apartment closer to Tré's school in North Richland Hills, but it didn't keep Nate out of our lives. It was like he was a demonic force, always oppressing me. He bothered us constantly and seemed to enjoy making me miserable. He told me he wanted to see the kids more. I had begun graduate school two nights a week and told him he could be with the boys on those two nights—which lasted for one semester before he grew tired of the responsibility.

When he decided to move to Georgia, I was glad to see him go, but he continued to call and harass me. "I can't believe you divorced me!" he'd say. "You're gonna pay for this, and I can't afford no $2,000 a month child support, so you're gonna have to figure out something else."

The house had not sold. Nate was out of money and growing desperate to find some cash. He lowered the price of the house to $650,000 and called to tell me I'd better agree to any offers. I did agree. Whatever the house sold for, I would be fine. Things would work out. I knew I would also receive a portion of Nate's retirement. This included a small settlement now and eventually a portion of his 401(k) when he reached retirement age. So I decided to stop renting and build a new house.

I knew I needed to be close to Ingrid so she could help me with the kids when I went back to work. We looked for the least expensive spot we could find in Southlake. I wanted to build my house close to hers. I had to take Tré out of Fort Worth Christian School because I could no longer afford the tuition.

He loved the school, and taking him out was an extremely difficult decision. It felt as though Tré was being penalized because
of the divorce. It didn't seem fair.

In May, Nate served me with papers. He took me to court to
get joint custody of the children and wanted out of the $2,000
monthly child support payments. I would not agree to joint
custody. I wanted full custody of the children, and I didn't care
what he paid me in child support. He could pay whatever—so
he stopped paying support.

Now I was really in trouble—a single mom facing legal
battles and legal bills. I felt totally outclassed. Nate Newton was
still a celebrity, and everybody loved him. I was overwhelmed
even by the need to find an attorney. *Who could I trust? What
should I look for? How was I going to afford it?* I didn't know what
to expect or where to turn for help. The bills were staggering,
unbelievable. I was on my own.

By July, our new house was finished, and it felt like we
were finally beginning to turn a corner. Tré was twelve and
about to be baptized; King was ready to celebrate a birthday;
and we were moving into our very own home! We had a huge
celebration. At last, we seemed to be finding our own way. We
just had to make it through the custody battle.

When I arrived at the first court appearance, I was escorted
into a mediation room. I was asked to explain why I didn't
want to let my boys go to Georgia with Nate. I explained that
they would be in danger. I told the mediators that something
was wrong with Nate, that he had a violent temper. I told them
about the dogs he kept in Georgia—pit bulls. "The kids won't
be safe," I said in earnest. "Nate is not stable. It will not be good
for the boys to go to Georgia."

"Can you prove he's not fit?" they asked.

I described some of the things that happened in our marriage—about the violence and abuse.

"Did he ever hurt the children?"

"No," I said with a sigh, "he never hurt the children, but he is violent."

"That has nothing to do with him not being able to take care of the kids," came the reply.

I was stunned when the mediators told me I had to allow Nate visitation rights, which meant thinking about such things as which holidays the children would spend with him. Then the subject of child support came up. Because Nate no longer had an income, he was no longer obligated to pay the amount that had been agreed upon for child support. Once again, everything was coming out in Nate Newton's favor. *Will I ever be free of this man? Even now, he gets to call all the shots.*

I left the courthouse dejected. I thought about reaching out to friends, but I wasn't used to sharing my problems with people. Even if I did call someone, what could they do? How could they help? I was used to trying to figure things out on my own and didn't know how to ask for help. God was the only one I really trusted. I had trouble with trust even in my closest relationships. All I knew to do was pray.

On November 4, 2001, Nate was arrested in St. Martin Parish, Louisiana. The police had discovered 213 pounds of marijuana in his van, but there was no conviction. I continued to pray. I was desperate to find a way to prevent the boys from going to Georgia with Nate.

In December, we had our next child custody court appointment. I had paid more than $40,000 in legal fees and was at the end of my rope. I fasted and prayed. "Please, God," I prayed, "intervene." I called my friend Sheila and asked if she could come to court to stand with me. She immediately agreed. When the mediator asked me which holiday Nate could have the boys, I said, "New Year's Day."

I looked across the courtroom. There was Nate and his girlfriend. He was smiling and hugging her. Our eyes met, and my heart sank. It seemed as if he took pride in hurting me. I thought about all the things I had been through with him. I had never done anything to tarnish his reputation. I stood by him whenever he was in trouble. I took care of him and lived with his abuse in silence. I watched him lavish gifts on others, while all I got were angry words and curses. *Why did he have to take the boys too?*

There was just one more court appearance to get through, and then everything would be settled. I left the courthouse brokenhearted. All I could do was surrender the future to God. "It's up to you now, God," I prayed. A few days before our fortieth birthdays in December—just five weeks after Nate's arrest in Louisiana—Nate once again made national headline news. He was caught with 175 pounds of marijuana on Interstate 45. This time, however, he was not released; he was convicted and sentenced to thirty months in a federal prison.

Tré was devastated. He had just started in a public school, so he was away from the friends he'd grown up with and the support structure he had come to depend on. I was embarrassed and angry. It was a nightmare.

CHAPTER 26

Standing Strong

Vitality shows in not only the ability to
persist but in the ability to start over.

F. Scott Fitzgerald

If my kids are going to survive this, I'm the one who is going to have to show them how to do it. I looked at myself in the mirror, measuring the reflection I saw. Instead of sadness, I saw determination. I saw hope—even confidence. "We're going to make it," I said out loud, lifting my chin. I twisted the tube of lipstick and applied the color. I nodded to myself and squared my shoulders. "Better."

The boys and I grew even closer in the days that followed. I didn't ask for help. I had a fiercely independent streak in me, and I believed we could deal with things on our own. I didn't allow the boys to watch television during the week, and we had Bible study every day. We were active in church and spent lots of quality time together—healing, coping, finding our way. I got involved in women's ministry and began looking for a job. I had not been employed professionally for some time, and I knew I needed something more than an entry-level position to take care of our needs.

I really needed the child support, but with Nate in prison, there was none. Even with careful management, paying the legal fees and apartment rental costs and then building a house had exhausted all my resources. I felt like I needed to stay home with the boys during the transition, but I began to amass credit card debt just to make ends meet. That was something I was not willing to continue. It was time to take a job—any job. Even if it wasn't enough to sustain us, it would be income.

A friend, an internist, knew I needed a job and got me an

interview at the clinic where he worked. I was hired for a position in the medical billing department. It was an entry-level position. The salary wasn't enough to meet our expenses, and the job responsibilities weren't challenging, but it was a job. It was also close to home, which allowed me to remain accessible to my kids. I took it, praying that God would make my income stretch and grant me favor.

Three months after I began working, a management position opened up at the clinic. I spoke with the lead physician at the clinic, telling him I was interested and qualified. But in the back of my mind, I was concerned about all the bad publicity surrounding Nate's arrest and afraid that because of it, I might not be given a fair shot at the job. My worries turned out to be unfounded. This compassionate man asked me to tell him about the kind of person I was. He asked about my experience and how I could be an asset to the company. I answered his questions openly and honestly.

"You are the person I'm interested in," he said. "I'm not interested in who you've been married to or what the media has to say about you. I will not judge you, nor will I penalize you for someone else's actions. All I ask is that you remain focused while you're here and not let that life interfere." From that time on, my career blossomed.

⌒⌒

While Nate was serving his sentence, he often called and sent letters, repeatedly asking to see the kids. I wasn't sure what to do. *Should I keep the boys away from their father? Should I take them to visit Nate and expose them to prison? What's best for them? What's best for me?* I honestly didn't know what to do.

Tré missed his father and was old enough to understand that Nate had broken the law and was serving time as punishment.

King was still young enough that he didn't understand anything about the situation, but he also missed his daddy and kept asking to see him. I had reservations about exposing the boys to prison, but I felt sorry for Nate and was heartbroken for the boys.

I decided that keeping the boys away was selfish, and so I committed to taking them to Texarkana once a month to visit Nate in prison. I had no idea what to expect. As the date for our first visit drew near, I longed for someone to talk to who could prepare me for the experience. I could think of no one, so once again, I prayed about it. I was scared to death as I made the long drive, but I knew God was with me—watching, guiding, protecting. I hoped that seeing Nate in jail would not disturb the boys.

Visitation took place on Sunday, and it was too far to drive there and back in one day, so we drove over on Saturday and spent the night in a hotel. The first visit with Nate was awkward and strange, but Tré seemed relieved to be able to see with his own eyes that his dad was okay. King was more interested in the playground out front, but Nate seemed glad to see him. We made the long drive home, and I put the boys to bed. I went to my room and collapsed on the bed, completely drained.

This became our monthly routine until the last year of Nate's sentence when he was transferred to a prison in Louisiana. The Monday mornings after our trips were difficult. We were all so tired. Mornings were already hard. Tré had to be on the field for football practice at 6:30 a.m. Every day, I had to wake up five-year-old King, put him in the car, and drive Tré to practice. Then I drove back home, got King fed and ready for school, and went to work.

For all the years I was married, I'd never had to worry about money. Nate gave me what I needed for monthly household bills. If the kids needed clothes or shoes or fees for any of their activities, he gave me his credit card to take care of it. When I scheduled his appearances, I received a small percentage for my work, and that took care of my personal needs, which were never much. Now I thought about money all the time. I had to be super-frugal. Every month, I had to manage and balance, and then adjust and balance again. Even though it was a fight to survive, it felt like a light load in comparison to what I had lived through. I gladly dealt with financial issues in exchange for peace of mind and safety. My heart was filled with gratitude that God had brought me through.

For the most part, our friends didn't want to talk about Nate's situation, and we didn't volunteer any information. I believe we wanted to open up and share what we were going through—we just didn't know how. We didn't know where to begin! Even with caring people all around us, it sometimes felt as though we stood alone in our past and in our pain. It was our burden to bear. It was our responsibility to deal with.

I knew God wanted to do great things through me and the boys. I wanted us to focus on others and not get bogged down in our troubles and what we were dealing with when it came to our experiences with Nate. We got involved in Presbyterian Night Shelter in Fort Worth, supported food drives and clothing drives, and were actively involved in reaching out to others.

Tré was now fourteen and held a Bible study in our home. He was a phenomenal athlete and an outstanding student. Though he was quiet, he was friendly and open about his faith. Instead of turning bitter when things were hard or allowing the trauma experienced in his childhood to overwhelm him, he excelled in everything he did. I was immensely proud of him.

King was seven, and he and Tré were close. Tré was very protective of King and became his hero. King loved watching Tré play football. He followed him around and listened to him. Disciplining King was never a problem for me when Tré was around.

Tré's high school team, the Southlake Carroll Dragons, was a championship-caliber team, and his games were always exciting to watch. One night, I was sitting in the stands cheering him on and visiting with other football moms, when out of nowhere—*there was Nate!* He had been released from prison and wanted to surprise us. I had not heard from him in months. Now here he was, looking like a wild man—and he'd brought the woman he was with the night I called the police to make him leave our property. I knew the time for his release was approaching, but I hadn't given it much thought. I was completely shocked!

After the game, Nate found Tré, and they talked for a while. My friends just kept looking at me, perhaps for an explanation, but no one said anything. I'd never talked to any of them about Nate, and I certainly didn't know what to say now. My thoughts were racing. *He's back. What does this mean? Is Nate going to leave us alone? Does he expect to come around the house now to visit the boys?*

It had been nearly three years since Nate left. While he was in prison, I felt completely safe, knowing he couldn't show up to bother us. I wasn't sure how to handle it now that he was back in Texas. It turned out that I didn't have to wait long to find out what it was going to mean having Nate nearby again. He asked if I was sure we weren't going to get back together again, and I assured him we would not. He said he wanted to retrieve all the belongings I had stored for him while he was gone, and then he wanted to take me back to court over custody.

"What is it you really want?" I asked him. "Surely you don't want joint custody of the boys. They are settled in their life. They are active in school. Tré is very involved in sports. Why would you want to interrupt their stability?"

There had been no child support during the entire time Nate was in prison. He didn't want to be responsible for back child support, and he wanted the monthly amount he was supposed to pay further reduced. I knew he didn't have any income—he didn't even have a job. We had gone all this time without any help from him, and I didn't care about that—all I wanted was custody.

Our attorneys argued back and forth, and we finally agreed that Nate would pay $850 a month to support the boys and 20 percent of the back child support over a period of time. I wondered if he had any idea how hard it had been on us financially while he was away. It didn't matter. He was giving me full custody, and we would stay out of court. That was what mattered. The boys would stay with me.

CHAPTER 27

Familiar Tune

Difficult things take a long time,
impossible things a little longer.

André A. Jackson

Yes, Nate was back.

While in prison, he was as active in the boys' lives as prison allowed him to be. Whenever he called, he was nice to us. He was interested in the details of their lives and expressed concern for them in his letters, so I was hopeful that things might be amiable between us now that he was back. But it wasn't to be. It seemed like every encounter with Nate was difficult and disagreeable. He was angry whenever he was around me. I didn't want his anger spilling out around the boys, so I avoided him as much as possible.

Now that I was working full-time, it was important to me that I focused on the boys whenever I spent time with them. I didn't take calls on my cell phone or answer email. When I was spending time with them, I gave them my full attention. My friends knew this and respected our family time.

One Sunday afternoon, I took King to his Little League baseball game. He was so cute in his uniform! I loved watching him play ball. Nate also came to watch. I kept my distance and sat with several other parents. Another little boy on the team was hitting home runs every time he got a turn at bat. He was having quite a streak! All the boys wanted to use his bat—after all, it must be the bat that was responsible for all those home runs. When it was King's turn to hit, he picked up the boy's trophy bat to give it a try. I was smiling from ear to ear as he took his turn at home plate.

Then I heard, "Dot!"

"Dot, what bat is that?" Nate shouted at me from across the stands.

I didn't answer. *What difference does it make? King is up. Watch the game*, I thought to myself.

"Dot!" Nate shouted again. "I said whose bat is he using?"

People around me got restless. I was embarrassed. *Why did Nate have to shout and make a scene? This was just Little League. Stop it!*

"I spent my f_____ money on a bat for King, and he's using someone else's bat? Why?" Nate ranted.

He continued shouting at me in front of everyone. I was mortified, and the parents in the stands were clearly getting uncomfortable. I couldn't bring myself even to look at Nate. I took out my cell phone and called Ingrid. "Hi, Ingrid," I said. "Can you come and sit with me at King's game?" I never called Ingrid during their family time, so when I called her on a Sunday afternoon, she immediately knew something was wrong.

"On my way," she said. She arrived within a few minutes and came to sit by me. Nate would not let it go. He was stirred up and kept demanding to know whose bat King was using and why wasn't he using the bat he had bought for him. It was awful.

King knew something was wrong. Throughout the game, he kept looking into the stands and hearing Nate yell at me.

When the game ended, I gave Ingrid a quick hug, and she looked me in the eyes, knowingly. I gathered King's things and hurried him along to the car.

"I *will* be talkin' to King!" Nate shouted as I drove away.

I called Tré. "Your dad's in a rage," I began. "I don't know what's going to happen, but as soon as I get home, I want you to take your brother upstairs. Your dad is following me home. I'm not going to let him in. I don't know what's going to happen."

When I pulled into the driveway, Nate was no longer behind

me. I hurried inside and sent King up to shower. *Maybe Nate decided not to come after all.* I hoped so. I let out a sigh of relief.

Bam-bam-bam! I jumped. Nate was pounding on the door.

"Let me in, Dot!" Nate shouted, still banging on the door.

"Don't let him in, Mama!" Tré called out from upstairs, "Don't let him in!"

I went to the door, double-checking to make sure it was locked.

Bam-bam-bam-bam-bam! Nate was pounding on the door so hard that I feared he would break the hinges and knock it down.

"If you pound on the door again, I am going to call the police. Do you hear me?" I shouted. "I will call the police. Go away. I'm not letting you in here like that."

"Dot, I just want to see the kids," Nate said much more calmly. "I want to apologize. Please, just let me in. I want to talk to King."

I stood there, my hand on the deadbolt. I hesitated.

"Mama, don't," Tré begged.

"I just want to apologize, Dot," Nate repeated.

King was on the stairs, crying. "Let him in, Ma; let him in. Please."

"King, baby . . ." I began.

"Ma, please, he just wants to talk to me," King pleaded, tears streaming down his cheeks.

Tré was shaking his head no. "Don't," he mouthed.

King was crying, and Nate was still pleading with me to let him in. Slowly, I turned the deadbolt and cracked the door. "You are going to be calm or I am going to call the police. Do you understand?" I knew if I called the police, it would mean a certain return to jail for Nate. He didn't have any room for a parole violation, so it gave me confidence that he would behave.

Nate pushed past me. "Tré, King," he called up the stairs, "come down here, boys."

Reluctantly, the boys came down the stairs, their faces betraying their apprehension.

"Nate," I warned, "you said you were coming in to apologize, remember?"

"I bought that bat," he said to King. "Why were you using someone else's bat?" His voice was very loud and thick with anger.

"This isn't working out," I said. "You're too mad to talk right now, and that doesn't sound like an apology. I think you better leave."

"Why were you using someone else's bat?" Nate shouted, and slammed his fist down on my marble table. The table broke.

"Get out!" I shrieked. "Get out, *now*!"

I opened the door and gestured for him to leave. "*Now!*" I said. I was shaking uncontrollably.

Nate left. I shut the door, and King ran over and hugged me. Tré was furious.

"Why are we still having to deal with this?" he shouted as he punched the wall.

I had never seen him do anything like that, and it scared me. For the first time, I was scared for Tré. I saw the potential for anger to grab him like it had grabbed Nate, and I was terrified for him.

"Tré, baby," I said, crying. *Oh, God, why can't this be over?*

We'd had plans that night with Ingrid and Monte, but I was too upset to go to dinner. I called Ingrid and told her we couldn't come. I asked Monte if he would come over. Tré needed him.

Monte took Tré out and spent time talking to him, like he often did. Monte and Ingrid treated Tré like one of their own and gave him the opportunity to travel extensively with their family. It was good for the boys to be around functional, loving families—families with a mom and dad who respected each other, treated each other kindly, and poured out their love freely. I was very blessed to have these amazing people in my life. Monte spent lots of time with his boys, and I was grateful that he made time for mine too.

We also had Lynn and K-Mart. They had moved away in 1993 but returned in 2002, shortly after Nate and I were divorced. They found a house in nearby Keller and were wonderful friends to us, like family. Their son and Tré were just five days apart in age, and all I ever had to do was pick up the phone and they were quick to help out with my boys. Any time I called, one of them would ask, "You bringing the kids over?" I never had to ask—it was like they knew I had a hard time asking for help, so they made it easy on me and just offered.

There were more angry episodes with Nate. Even in public, he was quick to verbalize his anger and speak to me disrespectfully. He often showed up for the kids' sporting events, which were mostly the times when they saw him. It was never nice between us, though. It seemed like just being around me stirred up the worst inside of Nate. Whatever he felt toward me, he didn't know how to express it in any way except anger.

CHAPTER 28

Give and Receive

There is nothing on this earth more to
be prized than true friendship.

Thomas Aquinas

It was August 2005. We were active members of our church and had made many wonderful friends there. Tré was involved in youth group; I led Bible studies; and things in our family had settled into a comfortable routine. Nate was still the wild card, and we never knew exactly what to expect, but we had learned how to deal with things, and we were strong and stable.

My extended family still lived in Buras, Louisiana, sixty miles south of New Orleans, where I grew up. When Hurricane Katrina hit in August that year, my mother, siblings, and aunts and uncles lost everything. There was nothing left, so the entire family took refuge at my house.

For the next three weeks, Tré, King, and I shared our home with seventeen people. It was total chaos. They sat up all night, glued to news reports, trying to find out about the damage. As dawn approached, one by one they fell into restless, fitful sleep. Their days and nights were completely backward. They were in shock, trying to cope with the loss of their property and personal belongings. Time stood still for them.

The boys were in school, and I was working every day. Every square inch of our home was occupied. The bathroom was never empty. There were pillows and blankets and clothes and shoes strewn everywhere. Just making sure there was enough food to feed everyone was a full-time effort. I had tremendous support from my church and from friends. They donated money for food and clothing, and the church helped us get my relatives into temporary apartments or houses. We received donations of cash and groceries, and the organization I worked for helped out by providing free health care. We also needed help with transportation. Friends pitched in to shuttle everyone to agencies to replace essential documents. They needed absolutely everything, including birth certificates, social security cards, and bank records—everything had been destroyed in the storm. It was a nightmare.

The whole family was trying to figure out what to do next. The news was on all the time. Every moment of any broadcast about the storm damage found them watching in horrified attention. I felt their sadness and anxiety and wanted to help in any way I could. But there was lots of laughter too. The circumstances were horrible, but having my family around was wonderful.

My family is resourceful. They researched sources of help and were able to access available supplies. I was proud of them. They didn't give up, and they didn't quit. I saw their strength and admired their tenacity. Eventually, everyone moved back to Louisiana to rebuild and start again. Only my mom decided to remain in Texas. She moved nearby, and I was glad she stayed.

Once again, I was reminded that no matter what we have to endure, we can live a blessed life. God surrounds us with a blanket of love. He touches every area of our lives and makes sure we have exactly what we need. Even when things are bad—in the valley of the shadow—he is with us. He is always with us.

During Tré's junior year of high school, he started looking at colleges, and colleges started looking at him. He was an amazing athlete, and several schools expressed interest and made offers. He wasn't interested. Tré would not settle. He was determined to attend either the University of Texas at Austin (UT) or Notre Dame, but all he had gotten from them was an invitation to visit their campus on their Junior Day. After arriving at UT for Junior Day, we signed in at the registration table, and a little while later, we were summoned to Coach Mack Brown's office for a personal chat. At the end of our chat, Coach Brown offered Tré a scholarship to play football at UT. We had no idea they were even interested in Tré—and here they were offering him a full scholarship while he was just a junior in high school!

Tré wanted his dad to be part of his decision, and he asked Coach Brown if he could call Nate and talk to him about it. "Of course," Coach said.

Tré called Nate and asked him if he would be interested in coming to Austin to see the place and give his input, and Nate drove for three hours to meet us on campus. When he arrived, he and Tré talked about the offer, going over the pros and cons. My main goal that day was to find out more about the faculty and staff Tré would spend time with and whether he would be positively influenced both academically and spiritually. Football was definitely Nate's area of expertise. I felt it was best to defer to him in decisions related to where Tré would get the best football opportunity. I would have been happy with any choice Tré made.

Tré decided to accept the scholarship, which he did that same day. When we returned home from the UT visit, we canceled a planned trip to visit Notre Dame. In Tré's heart, the University of Texas had been his first choice. There wasn't a need to look any further.

Tré graduated in December 2007, a full semester early. He was eager to begin college and didn't want to wait, so in January 2008, he began his studies at the University of Texas.

This was a difficult time for King. He was in the sixth grade when Tré left for college, and everything changed for him. Tré's leaving was hard for both of us. We had become an inseparable family unit and cared deeply about each other. We loved each other. When Tré left, an emptiness hung over the house. Nothing was quite the same.

One of King's teachers gave him an assignment to write about something that affected his life. King wrote about Tré leaving home to go to college. He talked about Tré being the person he looked up to for everything and how he was his best friend. It took King a long time to adjust to Tré being in college. Somehow, it didn't feel quite right being just the two of us. Something was missing.

One evening I had dinner with my friend Rayne. She said to me, "Dorothy, I see you reach out to a lot of people. You have helped me through a very difficult time in my life, but I don't feel like I know anything about you."

I froze. I hadn't expected this.

"How do I get to know you?" she asked. "You never share anything about yourself. How can I find out more about you? Can you be open and honest with me? I want to have a transparent relationship so I'll know what you need as much as you know what I need."

Rayne and I had been friends for a long time, and her observation surprised me. I was also touched that she was offering this kind of close friendship to me and felt overwhelmed by her generosity of spirit.

"I feel stuck," I began, pausing, not sure if I should continue. "Right now, things are very strange in my life. There are things I believe I need to talk to someone about, but it is really hard for me to trust people. It isn't that I don't love you . . ."

"You hurt me when you won't let me help you." Rayne said. "You are always giving, but you are not willing to receive. You won't let me in. Quite a few people have noticed that you have a wall built around you. As nice as you are, as giving as you are, you won't let anybody inside your space."

"It's hard for me to trust," I said. "But I want to. Will you be patient with me? I need time to figure things out."

After my conversation with Rayne, I thought about my cousin Scarlette. Until Hurricane Katrina, she was the only family who lived near me in Texas. She was a single mom who was raising two girls, Ariel and Whittney, on her own. I couldn't remember a single time she had asked for my help. She was an incredibly strong woman. She went back to school and got her degree while raising her daughters by herself. I was proud of her. Though I felt close to her, and I would have been privileged and pleased to help her with the girls, she had never reached out to me for assistance. Maybe this difficulty — this inability to ask for help — was part of our family's culture.

As I thought about it more, I realized that my desire to never be a burden to anyone had led me to close myself off, which ultimately made it difficult to seek support, even when I needed it most. I knew I needed to learn how to receive. I needed to learn that asking for help is not a sign of weakness, but it's a way to give others an opportunity to be a blessing. For the first time, I considered that the ability to receive from others was not somehow of less value than the ability to give to them.

CHAPTER 29

Perfect Love

Greater love has no one than this, than to
lay down one's life for his friends.

John 15:13 NKJV

During Tré's senior year of high school, I had often visited Gateway Church in Southlake, Texas. I loved hearing Pastor Robert Morris preach. I would attend Saturday night services at Gateway and then attend our church on Sunday mornings. I was drawn to Gateway, but as long as Tré was at home, I didn't want to disrupt things for him. Now that he was in college, I felt like I had a green light to begin attending Gateway regularly.

At the time, Gateway Church was much smaller than it is now, and Pastor Robert always mingled with the congregation after services. One Sunday, I was visiting with Arnita and Mike Taylor, who were friends of Pastor Robert. He came over to where we were standing and introduced himself to me. Nate had told me a few days previously that he'd had a conversation with Pastor Morris, so I said, "It is so good to meet you. Just last week, Nate mentioned he had seen you and had a chance to visit."

"Oh," he said, "so you're Dorothy, Nate Newton's ex-wife? My wife, Debbie, would love to meet you."

"I'll give Dorothy's number to Debbie," Arnita offered.

The next day, Debbie Morris called, and we set a lunch date. This began a series of lunch dates a few times a year. We didn't get to visit together very often, but when we did, it was an extra-special time for me. Debbie was soft-spoken, tender, kindhearted, gentle—a beautiful example of a godly woman. The church was growing rapidly, and her schedule was very full, so I was careful to respect her time. We texted each other often and managed to stay in touch.

I always assumed the reason we were friends was that she needed a safe place. By now, Pastor Robert was well-known nationally and internationally, and I knew what it was like to be the wife of a famous husband. I figured Debbie had reached out to me because she needed a friend who was interested in her for herself, not because of who she was married to. I knew all too well what that was like, and I wanted to be a good friend to her, whatever that looked like. Trusting people is very difficult when you've got a famous husband.

It was the end of February 2008, and Debbie and I were enjoying one of our first lunches together in the new year. We had visited for nearly two hours when she said, "Dorothy, I know you're involved in a lot of things, but what is your passion?"

I paused for a moment, wondering if I should share what was going on inside of me. "Well," I began, "as of January, I decided to completely erase my calendar. I have been involved in so many things, and I just don't want to do them anymore." I took a sip of tea. My stomach felt like it had butterflies inside.

"I feel stuck, Debbie," I continued. "The place I am in right now feels foreign to me. From the time I was a little girl, I felt close to God—like I could always feel him hugging me, and I was hugging him back. It was always personal and intimate. Now, for the first time in my life, I can't feel him." I looked across the table at her, and her attention was completely focused on me.

"I have never felt so stuck spiritually, like I can't grow. For the first time, I don't want to lead a Bible study. I don't want to feed the homeless. I don't even want to go to lunch or spend time with friends. I have no desire to meet their spiritual needs or pray for them. To answer your question, *people* have always been my passion, and now I no longer have a desire to reach out to them. I just feel numb."

Debbie sat there quietly, not interrupting, keeping a steady, loving gaze on my face. She smiled, encouraging me to continue, without saying a word.

"I've always looked forward to opportunities to minister. I have ministered to so many people in the past. Many of them mentioned that they sought professional help. Maybe I need a counselor ... I don't know. I'm not sure. I think right now I'm just going to be still and wait. God will reveal it to me."

"Well, Dorothy, if you want to see somebody," she offered, "I have someone I trust that I think you would enjoy knowing and visiting with." I looked at her, knowing she was sincere.

"I don't know, Debbie," I said, suddenly feeling cautious. "I'll be honest with you, I have some trust issues. The life I've lived—it's hard for me to know who I can trust." The faces of all the people I had trusted and then been betrayed by flashed across my mind. I had been disappointed too many times.

"Actually, the worst in my life is over," I said, trying to strike a more hopeful note. "It is in my past. I don't really think I need to talk to anybody. I was just thinking about it, that's all. I haven't really decided to do that. I'm fine."

"Let's pray about it," Debbie suggested. "I have someone in mind you would really enjoy talking to. Her name is Rebecca. I love her, and I trust her. I believe she can help you, Dorothy."

She smiled again. Everything about her reflected the peace and love of God.

"So, I guess that explains what your passion is," she said.

"Right," I said. "Nothing. Nothing is my passion right now."

"Think about it," she said, sipping her tea. "I believe the Lord has a lot planned for you. This would be something good for you."

"Are you gonna be there with me?" I asked.

"Yes," she said, "if that's what you want, I'll be there with you. If you decide you want to see her, I'll come with you."

Lunch was over. I always enjoyed lunch with Debbie, but we didn't do it often. I knew it would be months before I saw her again. We would send text messages and stay in touch, but I was thinking, *Yeah, right. Debbie doesn't have time to check into this. She has a million things to do. She travels with Pastor Robert. She's not going to check into this.*

Remember, I said to myself, *this is not about you. You are here for her; you're not here to be needy.* In truth, I cared about her very much. I wanted her to have a friend she could lean on and trust. The last thing I wanted was to be someone else she needed to expend energy on. I felt somewhat remorseful for even sharing my problem with her.

Thirty minutes after leaving the restaurant, my phone rang. I pulled it from my purse and looked at the screen—it was Debbie.

"Dorothy," she said, "I checked with Rebecca, and she has three dates open." She listed all the dates and times. "Which one is good for you?"

"Debbie," I said, "I'm surprised you called, but ... wait ..."

"I'll hold on while you decide," she said, not giving me a chance to back out. The excitement in her voice was unmistakable. Quiet, sweet Debbie was bubbling on the other end of the line.

"Okay, let me look," I said.

"If you still want me there, I'll be there," she reassured me. "What day is best for you?"

Pink Impact, Gateway's annual conference for women, was just a few weeks away. I checked my calendar and picked a date after the conference.

I can't believe this, I thought to myself after I hung up. *I just can't believe it.* Debbie took the time to ask me what I was passionate about. She was genuinely interested in me. I wanted to be there for her, and here she asked about me, getting me to open up to her and share what was going on in my life.

I couldn't wrap my head around the fact that she had followed through that very same day—just thirty minutes later. I thought about the excitement in her voice and how authentic and real her attention to me had been.

The next time I saw my friend Lynn Martin, I told her, "I think I need to see a counselor, Lynn. I just feel stuck."

Lynn is a strong woman who loves God. Any time I went to her feeling down or dejected, she would look at me and say, "Snap out of it, Dot." Then she would remind me of how strong I was and tell me I was not a quitter—that I could get through this. This was often exactly what I needed. She was the "tough love" person in my life.

When I told her I was thinking about seeing a counselor, she said, "You don't need a counselor. All you need is God, the One you have been depending on your whole life. Who brought you through everything you've been through? God, right? Why do you need a counselor now?"

"I don't know, Lynn," I answered. "I've just been thinking about it, that's all."

Now I was wavering a little, not sure if I wanted to go through with the appointment, but not wanting to back out after Debbie had gone to so much trouble to pave the way.

A few days later, I saw Ingrid. When I told her I was thinking about seeing a counselor, without hesitation she said, "That's a very good thing. I always believed you should be able to talk to somebody. You've been through an awful lot. It will help."

On the day of my appointment, I was scared to death. I sat in my car, trying to talk myself into going inside to Rebecca's office. *Why did I agree to this?* I thought. *You know why*, I answered myself. I had prayed a great deal about this since my conversation with Debbie. I knew for sure I was supposed to do it, but I was nervous. I didn't know what to expect or what was expected of me. I had never seen a real counselor before — Nate and I saw one once for two sessions, but I never really counted that. I wasn't sure how I was supposed to act or what I was supposed to say.

I got out of the car, locked the door, and went inside. Debbie was already there, and I was grateful.

"Where would you like to sit?" Rebecca asked. Simple question, right? But I froze. *Should I choose the love seat or the chair?*

"Dorothy?" Debbie reached out her hand. "Where would you like to sit?"

At first, I wanted to sit next to Debbie on the love seat, close enough to hold her hand, because I was so afraid. But somehow I knew if I sat next to Debbie, I would be dependent on her. I wanted to be independent. *If this is going to work*, I thought, *I'm going to have to do it on my own. Debbie is not going to be able to come to every session with me.* I looked at the chair, standing there by itself—it was independent and strong, and it represented courage. I sat down in the chair.

Rebecca suggested we pray together, and that really helped me. She encouraged me to talk about anything I wanted to talk about. I assumed this was how it worked: I would tell her everything, and then she would tell me what I needed to do to fix it. I rushed through my whole life story as fast as I could, wanting to get it all out and be done with it. I talked fast, my nervousness causing me to speed up even more.

As I shared, tears welled up. *I cannot cry*, I told myself. *I cannot cry. If I start crying, I might not be able to stop.* That was the last thing I wanted. I swallowed hard and forced the tears back inside. I just wanted to get through this.

"Dorothy," Debbie said gently, "it's alright to cry."

"No," I said, shaking my head. "No, if I start, I won't be able to stop." I had not cried in a very long time. I believed I needed to be strong. I didn't believe I should take time crying over things I couldn't change.

As I continued sharing my story, so much pain came to the surface—more than I ever expected. I kept stopping to gain composure. It felt like the floodgates were trying to open, and I was terrified that if I allowed myself to cry, I wouldn't be able to stop.

I wanted to finish my story. I wanted to tell the whole thing in one session so I would never have to do it again. I didn't ever want to think about these horrible things again. I figured if I could get all this out, then the next time I came, Rebecca could tell me what I needed to do to fix things so I would no longer feel stuck.

When I finally finished, I looked at my watch—it had been almost three hours. I knew I had bounced around all over the place as long-buried memories came rushing out, but I had done it. I felt relieved.

"So, are you going to be able to help me?" I asked Rebecca. "Is this going to be a quick fix?"

Rebecca smiled at me and said, "Let God decide how long it's going to be. If you will commit, then I'm willing to do what-ever I can to be a vessel for God. I just need a commitment from you."

"What type of commitment?" I asked. I wasn't sure what she meant.

"Well, why don't we just schedule next week's visit," she

said, offering me no clue about the length of time we might work together or how many sessions we would have.

I was exhausted. I sat outside in my car for thirty minutes trying to compose myself. I could not believe I had just told a complete stranger my whole, painful life story.

I flipped down the visor, touched up my makeup, and took a deep breath. I had scheduled dinner that night with a friend who was going through a difficult divorce, and I needed to put myself back together. I shifted my focus to my friend and didn't give my experience with Debbie and Rebecca another thought. I was an expert at separating myself from painful things and dealing with the matters at hand.

The next week, I met with Rebecca again. Then we scheduled additional weekly meetings, but I wanted a quick fix. I wanted her to give me the steps to getting unstuck so I could follow them like a diet or exercise plan.

The problem was that I couldn't open up anymore. Rebecca encouraged me to talk about whatever I wanted to, but nothing came. I felt guilty about taking up this woman's time. *There must be other people she could help if I wasn't taking up the appointment time*, I thought. Session after session, I kept coming back, but I could not bring myself to open up again.

"I'm so sorry," I told Rebecca in one session. "I am wasting your time. It has been four weeks. You shouldn't be wasting your time on me because I'm going to be okay. I'm a strong person. I've been through terrible things, but that's all in my past. There are other people you can help. You must be impatient with me just showing up and not being able to talk about anything."

I was upset that I had dragged Debbie through my story. I was worried I might have damaged her as she sat through my entire spill. I wondered what she thought. *Would she judge me?*

Would she see me differently? I regretted that she knew my past. I wished I'd never agreed to come in the first place.

I genuinely felt like I had told Rebecca everything in our first conversation and there was nothing left to say. Taking up her time made me feel selfish and guilty. Every appointment was a major struggle. I didn't want to go, but God gave me no release. I showed up, but I wasn't engaged. I was resistant to everything. The more difficult I became, the sweeter Rebecca was. There seemed to be no end to her patience.

One afternoon, I came home from work on a day when I had a session scheduled for that evening. I prayed, "God, this is just not working out. It was sweet of Debbie, but nothing is happening. I'm wasting this woman's time. I feel guilty, and that is certainly not helping me feel less stuck. Other people need her. She can actually minister to them. I'm going to cancel. Okay?"

Nothing. I didn't hear a yes or a no—just nothing. I decided to take a long, hot bath and stay home. I would call Rebecca and cancel. I ran my bathwater and put in a CD that Gateway had given out for Mother's Day. It was a mix of music and voices reading Scripture. It relaxed me. I sunk down in the water, letting the Word wash over my soul. Wait—I recognized that voice! Right there on the CD was Rebecca's voice reading Scripture to me. I couldn't believe it. I could not escape!

I got out of the tub, got dressed as quickly as I could, and hurried to her office. "I know you want me to be there, God," I prayed. "I feel guilty, though. I don't understand the purpose for going. I don't want to go anymore. Help me know what to say to Rebecca tonight so I won't hurt her feelings when I tell her this is my last session."

I got to Rebecca's office and told her what happened in the tub. She smiled. It was a turning point. I can't explain it, but it was true.

Continuing with the sessions was the hardest thing I had ever done, but Rebecca was persistent. She was easy to talk to, even when what we talked about seemed totally irrelevant. *How could I not want to be here?* I thought. *Oh, well, I guess I'm not a quick fix after all.*

Session after session, Rebecca was consistent and patient. She never gave any indication that she was bored or tired of listening to me. It was a gift. For as long as I needed it, she was there. Other people would have given up on me long before now. And she wouldn't allow me to pay her. Rebecca had prayed about it, and God had told her there should be no exchange. He told her to minister to me from her heart, not for pay. If I had been paying her, I would already have spent thousands of dollars—and I knew I would have quit. God knew I needed Rebecca. For my entire life, I had always been the giver. I had never been the recipient of anything like this.

As my sessions with Rebecca continued, anger began to surface—anger that I had stuffed down and pushed away and convinced myself I didn't have. I was shocked by it. I was a Christian, and I loved the Lord. I wasn't supposed to feel like this. I had forgiven Nate, so where was all this anger coming from? It got to the point that my anger began to consume me. Every moment of my day, it was there with me—ugly, taunting, tempting me to explode. I was ashamed of it. I couldn't comprehend how I had lived for so long with all of it buried so deep, not even realizing how much space it had occupied in my subconscious.

To remain focused on my job and my care for King, I gave myself "containment time" during the day—time when I would allow anger to surface so I could deal with my issues. Then I would dutifully push it to the back of my mind so I could function.

One evening, I was in a session with Rebecca, but I was still holding things back. I didn't want to deal with one more ounce of anger. I believed I had talked about so much already that God would surely do whatever needed to be done in my life with what I had already shared. *Did I really need to bring up one more thing?* Then finally, breakthrough came.

I started to cry. First a few tears — then it was like a dam broke, and all the backed-up tears burst forth. I cried so much that I thought I would never be able to stop. I didn't realize there were so many tears inside of me that needed to be shed. It was a sweet release.

I had felt dirty from the moment I agreed to have sex with Nate before we were married. I had never felt pure and whole again from that night. I had suffered so much. I had compromised. I had made bad decisions. My boys had suffered. I had lived with shame.

As I cried, the tears cleansed me. God showed me that no matter what my life had been before, he could make it new again. The tears kept flowing. I felt completely poured out — emptied of all the guilt, sorrow, and shame. I was at last free to receive. It was as if the Holy Spirit took complete control over everything, and I was finally free. I didn't feel guilty anymore. I was overwhelmed by God's love. When the tears finally ended, I was completely spent — and completely at peace.

Rebecca prayed with me, and God showed me a vision of a girl in a plain, white dress. It was raining. I was in the mud, and my dress was getting dirty, yes, filthy. The weather got worse, and it turned into a storm with thunder and lightning. I cried out to God, and the rain stopped. Soaking wet, I looked up to the sky, and the clouds began to break. I twirled around and around, holding my arms up to God.

I looked up into his face and began thanking him, still

twirling. As I twirled around, my dress got beautiful. I got beautiful. Suddenly, there was no dirt anywhere, just green grass and sunshine and the Lover of my soul.

My entire body reverberated with gratitude. God loved me so much. I could feel him with every breath. I could sense him in every heartbeat. He had collected every one of my tears, and they were precious to him.

"Rebecca, can you see things pouring out of me?" I asked. "Can you see the joy? Can you see the love?"

It was then that I realized God did have great plans for me. I wasn't disqualified because of my past. My past did not define me. My whole life stretched out before me — a lot of living to do. I was God's vessel, pure and sanctified. I was holy, set apart for his perfect use.

I was free.

CHAPTER 30

New

And he that sat upon the throne said,
Behold, I make all things new.

Revelation 21:5

I was totally free from my guilty past. I no longer felt ashamed about the choices I had made. I thought I had forgiven Nate—I thought I had forgiven a lot of people—but I had much to learn about forgiveness. Most importantly, I had to learn to forgive myself and accept God's forgiveness without any strings attached. It was much deeper than emptying myself; it was God filling me, equipping me.

I had never walked away from God, even in the most difficult times of my life. My relationship with him had been strong, but it had been incomplete because I closed off part of myself, not allowing God's forgiveness to free me from shame. I had not received all he had to give. Now I freely surrendered every part of my heart, soul, and mind to him. We were inseparable, and I was filled with a joy overflowing.

For six months, I had met with Rebecca weekly. After the breakthrough came, we met less often. We spread out the sessions to every other week, then monthly, and finally, quarterly checkups. I was a completely different person. On April 1, 2010, I met with Rebecca for my quarterly checkup. It was a God-ordained meeting. During our session, my cell phone rang; it was my brother, Mike, calling. Mike and I hadn't grown up together, but we met when I was in college and had grown close over the years. My biological father was sick, and I had been making monthly trips to Maryland to visit him. Mike was calling to tell me our father had died.

In the past, when something tragic happened to me, I

pushed it down, dealing with it on my own and never sharing my pain with anyone. I got this terrible news while I was in the middle of my session with Rebecca. I talked with her about how I would handle it. I shared with her how close I had grown to my father. I had been given the opportunity to get to know him much better and had bonded with my brother and his family. I knew he was sick, but I had not expected him to die. Rebecca was there for me. She encouraged me to connect with Lynn and Ingrid and let them know how this affected me. I promised her I would.

The following day, I went to work and told no one. I didn't let anyone know how sad I was. But as I'd promised Rebecca, I called Ingrid and Lynn and asked them to go to church with me. Both agreed. On the way to church, I told them that my father died. It was the strangest feeling — I was not used to telling someone when I was hurting or in need. Ingrid and Lynn were wonderful. Even this small act was a breakthrough for me.

Things with Nate were much better now. I could see evidence of change in him. He was no longer angry when he saw me. We could be civil to each other in public settings, as well as in private. I knew he and his wife had gotten involved in church, and I prayed that the changes in him were genuine — that at last he had truly found the Lord. I hoped he was also living a new life. I forgave Nate in my heart for everything — I was free, and I wanted Nate to be free also. I wanted him to have a good relationship with Tré and King. They had made their peace with him and, I hoped, with their past. I truly wanted God's best for Nate Newton.

Tré had experienced several concussions in his years playing for the University of Texas. Nate and I flew to Austin and met with him and a team of doctors. Their advice was that Tré should no longer play football. We did our own research and found out as much information as we could. In the end, it was Tré's decision. He had information from his coaches, from the medical staff, and from us, but it was his decision to play or to give up football. Ultimately, he was the one who had to live with the choice, so we let him make it. In November 2010, he held a press conference and announced he would no longer play football.

The news was hard on the whole family. Tré had loved football since he was two years old. The only toys he ever wanted as a boy were footballs and little football men. He loved everything about the NFL. He loved watching Nate play and was proud that his daddy was a pro. He was also a scholar who was attending school on a football scholarship. Nate and I both supported his decision 100 percent. Tré told me he knew it would be selfish to continue playing. Another serious injury could leave him an invalid for life — and that would have meant I had to take care of him. He didn't want that for me.

Remarkably, UT honored his football scholarship. They did not penalize him because he was injured and unable to play. He continued to support the team, working with them and being involved from the sidelines. His passion for football had to express itself in other ways.

In February 2011, I received an invitation to attend WILD (Women in Leadership Development), a mentoring program offered through Gateway Church. The invitation indicated that all the meetings were held on weekdays. I was working full-time, so I knew I wouldn't be able to attend. I discarded the invitation without giving it much thought.

When my friend Holly asked if I had received an invitation to WILD, I told her I did but I dismissed it because of work. "Dorothy," she exclaimed, "do you realize how many women would give anything for an opportunity like this? This is special. You should at least pray about it."

I retrieved the invitation and forwarded it to my boss. It was a leadership class, and we were encouraged to attend classes that aimed to develop our leadership and management skills. "This class meets for two hours each week," I wrote in an email. "Would it be okay for me to attend?"

Seconds after I hit the Send button, the reply came back. "Absolutely!" it read. My last excuse was gone. I accepted the invitation.

CHAPTER 31

WILD

For to be free is not merely to cast off one's
chains, but to live in a way that respects
and enhances the freedom of others.

Nelson Mandela

I showed up for the first WILD class feeling a little shy. I wasn't really sure why I was here. I had always considered myself a leader, but there were just twenty-five people in the room, and I felt uncomfortable in such a small, intimate setting. The class facilitators began by asking each person to give her name and share something about herself. *Oh, no,* I thought. *I do not want to do this!* But I knew I was supposed to be there, so I did my best. And I ended up enjoying the class very much. The women were all really wonderful, and I was learning a lot.

Early on, Jan Greenwood, one of the teachers, announced that each member of the class would have to present a project at the end. This frightened me. *What kind of project?* Jan gave very few guidelines, and I preferred strict rules and expectations. The open-ended nature of the assignment made me uncomfortable. I also had a good idea of what my project was supposed to be, and that made me uncomfortable too.

Two years earlier, God had spoken to me and told me I was supposed to write my story. The next morning, I met Nate at a restaurant so he could drop off something for the boys. I told him, "Last night, God told me I was supposed to write a book." I even suggested to Nate that perhaps we should write it together. But I hadn't done anything about it since.

Over the next few weeks, I prayed in earnest about whether or not I should pursue writing my story as my class project. I asked a friend, Janet Gray, to pray about it with me. About a month later, I attended a function in Janet's new home, and she gave me a tour. One very small room was designated as her prayer closet. Inside, I noticed she had tacked up a picture of me with the boys, and next to it was a slip of paper with writing on it indicating she had been praying for us. In that moment, I felt I had confirmation that God was planning something great for me.

At the next class, Jan Greenwood asked if everyone was comfortable with their project and told us that if we weren't, we could ask her or one of the other teachers about it. After class, I approached her and said, "I don't want to miss the last class just because I don't want to do this project. I really appreciate the class. I will complete the assignment, and I don't mind sharing it with you, but I really don't want to share this with everyone."

"What is it?" Jan asked.

"It's a book overview," I said.

"Does God want you to write the book?" she asked.

"Yes," I said, "I know for sure that I'm supposed to write the book."

"Then why won't you be obedient?"

I stood there looking at her, thinking, *You don't even know me. Why are you talking to me this way?*

"Listen," she said, "God isn't asking you to write a bestseller, He just wants you to be obedient."

She was calling me out. She was so serious.

"I don't know why I am being this firm with you, but I need to tell you that God wants to use you and that you need to be obedient." She didn't say another word after that. I left feeling a little mad at her. *You don't have to be so mean*, I thought.

On the day I was to present my overview in class, I arrived forty-five minutes early and sat in my car praying. "Do not fear," I clearly heard God say to my heart. "I will be with you. Not just today either, but every day for the rest of your life. You are a vessel. I have purposed and planned your life, and this book is by my design."

I was flooded with total peace. *I could do this!*

When my turn came, I stepped up front and gave the overview. When I was finished, everyone applauded. "Thank you," I said. "I was happy to be obedient." I caught Jan's eye, and she smiled and nodded her approval.

A few weeks after the class ended, Jan contacted me and said she felt God was prompting her to start a writers group. She asked if I'd be interested. "Sure," I said, not expecting anything to materialize.

I had been obedient and completed the project. I stood in front of a roomful of people and shared some dark and painful parts of my story. This had been a big step for me, and I was ready to let it go. But it wasn't long until I received an email from Jan announcing that the writers group was a go and inviting me to attend. We met once a month on Monday evenings for six months. Jan provided great information, and it was a good class. I began making progress on the actual writing process, but I still felt like I didn't really know what I was doing.

One week, Jan arranged for a guest speaker named Wendy Walters to come to our meeting. In addition to giving practical information about writing and publishing, she asked each of us to tell her about our projects. She was full of energy and affirmed that what each of us had to share was unique and important. Then she gave us simple, straightforward action steps to follow through on. By the end of the evening, the room was bursting with creative energy, and each of us found ourselves thinking, *I can do this!*

A week later, I called Wendy to set up an appointment to meet with her. From that very first meeting, our conversation never felt like business. It was like we were old friends talking about next steps to push my project along. She willingly shared with me what she knew about writing and the publishing process, even recommending other people who might be a better fit to help me with my project.

I didn't want anyone else. I knew she was the one I wanted to work with. We set up another appointment, and I started from the beginning. She asked me questions and listened attentively, taking notes as I shared my story. This book you are reading right now is the result of our collaboration. God brought me everything I needed to accomplish the task he assigned to me. He's like that. When I obeyed and took steps of faith, God provided all the resources — people, time, finances, opportunities, strategy — every single thing needed to complete the task that came from his hand. All I had to do was obey.

Now you know my story. The way I did things didn't always match up with the way God intended. He wants us to have relationships. He loves people, and he gives us people to love and be loved by. I believed I was supposed to be strong and independent. I thought asking for help was a sign of weakness, or that it meant I wasn't relying on God. I didn't open up to anyone — and that was a mistake.

I wish I had sought help long before I did. I wish I had gone to the authorities. I wish I would have told my family about the danger I was in. I wish I had trusted Ingrid and Monte, Lynn and K-Mart — somebody. I didn't have to suffer as long as I did. What I experienced in my relationship with Nate was not punishment for my sins or my poor choices; it was abuse.

Looking back, I see how I actually enabled Nate. By staying with him and not forcing him to be accountable for his actions, I enabled his destructive behavior to continue. I put my children in a terrible situation. I was afraid—afraid for my life, afraid of being alone, afraid I wouldn't be able to provide for the boys without Nate's help.

At first, the abuse was verbal. Horrible arguments that lasted for hours. Cursing, intimidation, demeaning language. I wish I had reached out then and not allowed it to go any further. But it did go further. The verbal abuse became physical abuse and got worse by degrees over time. Then the physical abuse turned to sexual abuse. Nate was bigger than me and much stronger than me. I felt completely helpless to escape. I believed no one could stop the abuse. I believed that law enforcement authorities would give Nate a pass for his celebrity status. I didn't think anyone was capable of helping me escape, but I was wrong.

Fifteen years have passed since Nate and I were divorced in 2000. By no means can I say that I walk in that perfect freedom every day. There are times when the shadow of my past still tries to bring darkness to my soul. The difference now is that I recognize it and cast it off. I know how important it is to have people in my life to be accountable to—people I can be open with and trust not to betray me. Trust still doesn't come easily. I wish I could say it did, but God is still at work, and I know he will bring me into his perfect design.

I celebrate my story—every part of it. If I were given the opportunity to go back and change things, of course I would. But I am the person I am today as a result of the journey I have traveled. My strength and grace are a result of life lived and lessons learned.

I am stepping into a new chapter of my life—a chapter I hope will offer freedom to other women who are in abusive situations. Perhaps that describes you. If so, I pray that as you read my words, you realize that abuse of any kind is wrong. Abuse is never deserved and should never be tolerated.

I pray that abusers will recognize they are hurting the people they love the most and that they need help. They need God. They need accountability. They need someone to guard them and help them through their anger and bitterness and to resolve not to resort to violence.

God offers hope to us all. He provides a way of escape when we are ensnared in a trap that is outside his design. We each have a purpose. We each have a reason to live. I pray that my story will offer you hope for a new day. I pray that my experience will touch others and cause them to reach out for help and refuse to remain one day longer in the prison of abuse.

Mostly, I pray that my story will honor God. He is my everything. His love and his light have guided and protected me, even when I walked a path he did not choose for me. He has restored my soul, delivered me from the pit, and set my feet upon a solid rock. If you don't already, I pray you will come to know him as I do. I pray you will allow yourself to feel his love and accept his complete, total forgiveness and restoration.

He sees your tears. He hears your cry. He knows every detail of your life—even the things you think no one else sees or hears. He captures your every tear. There is hope. He will save you. Only believe.

Afterword

It's been nearly eight years since I completed the overview of this book for my WILD class, and more than three years since the book's first edition was published. Reading my story for the first time was a shock for many family members and friends. It is a fairly common trait among those who have been abused not to divulge everything that transpires during the course of an abusive relationship, and I had withheld the worst of it from most people. Since I've shared my story publicly, I've had many in-depth conversations with family members and friends in which I've tried to explain how the abuse happened and what it meant for me over the years.

It has taken considerable time to work through the pain—and I am by no means fully healed. In fact, I believe I am in a state of constant healing, and that I'm on a journey that will continue for the remainder of my life on earth. I'm not sure I'll ever reach the point of feeling totally healed and complete, but that's okay. I know I have God's grace to fill in the gaps, and I trust that his promise is true: He will continue the good work he has begun in me.

Nate and I continue to be cordial for the sake of our boys, each of whom has his own relationship with their father. Tré received a master's degree from the University of Texas in December 2013. He is currently employed there in the athletics fund-raising department. King recently completed high school. He earned an athletic scholarship to the University of Texas, San Antonio, and began his freshman year there in 2015.

I still enjoy my work at a health care organization, and in 2014, I completed my graduate studies, earning an MBA in Leadership. I volunteer in several capacities at Gateway Church, speak on various topics at business and women's conferences, and serve as an adviser on the board of The Life of a Single Mom Ministries. King and I served together for two years with SASO (Scholars and Athletes Serving Others) and also with the Dallas/Fort Worth chapter of Jack and Jill of America. I also enjoy being asked to serve as an occasional cohost on "Joni Table Talk," a Christian talk show on the Daystar Television Network.

My plans for the future haven't changed much. I strive to be the best parent I can possibly be to my boys. I work hard to be a servant leader, remaining obedient to God's calling on my life. I am an ordinary person with an extraordinary mission, which I think is true for all of us. We are meant to use the power of our words and actions to bring love and healing to others. All of us can and should be advocates for abuse victims, helping them to find and experience the physical, emotional, and spiritual transformation that takes place when our hope is placed in God.

Meet Nate Newton

Success isn't permanent, and failure isn't fatal.

Mike Ditka

When I began writing *Silent Cry*, it was important to me to give readers a look into not only Nate Newton's past but also his present. My objective was never to expose juicy details about a famous athlete, but to shine a light on domestic violence in hopes of helping others escape it and find healthy and meaningful lives on the other side. To that end, I arranged for my friend and collaborator, Wendy Walters, to interview Nate and learn more about the man he has become. This is what she wrote after interviewing Nate in 2011:

The weather was miserable the chilly October evening I met Nate at a Starbucks in Southlake, Texas. We had never met before, and as Nate entered the café, he scanned the room, looking for the person he was supposed to meet. I could see he was dressed in warm clothes in anticipation of standing outside to watch his son King play football for the Carroll High School Dragons later that evening.

I caught his eye and stood to meet him. "Nate?" I asked, not positive it was him. He'd lost considerable weight and looked very different from the photos I had seen when researching him on the Internet. "Yes, ma'am," he said, shaking my outstretched hand and sizing me up. This was definitely not his first interview.

I gestured to a corner where I had positioned some chairs to face each other in an attempt at privacy. I was grateful Nate had granted the interview and knew he was fully aware of the content of Dorothy's book. I could only imagine how he felt about the information soon to come to light. As a high-profile alumnus of the Dallas Cowboys, a well-known member of the Dallas/Fort Worth community, and a current radio personality (The Coop and Nate Show, 103.3, ESPN Radio), Nate is no stranger to public scrutiny of his personal life. Years of fame and infamy stretch behind him like yard lines on a familiar field.

As I prepared for our meeting, I came across words he'd spoken in another interview: "I don't care what you write about me. What I did, I did. That's on me." Other reporters have found him bluntly honest without any attempt to gloss over his missteps along the way. I was curious to know how he would respond to my questions. I began by telling him the purpose of my interview was not to dredge up his past, but rather to offer a perspective on his future. I wanted others who had been abusers to understand that the cycle of abuse does not have to continue indefinitely. There is hope.

"Let me first tell you something about my past," Nate began. "I always lived life to what I thought was the fullest for me. I'm an emotional person. I'm excitable. If I believe I'm right, I don't care what nobody say—how dumb it is or how dumb it may seem to somebody else—if I believe I'm right, that's the end of the story. My highs are very high; my lows are very low. That's what drove me, and sometimes I took things to extremes."

He took a sip of his coffee and settled in. He was ready to talk.

"My Uncle Charles died when I was in high school or college—I can't exactly remember when," he said. "When I would visit him, he always told me, 'Son, live life to the fullest. Live it how you want to live it.' Well, I took that beyond what he meant. He meant for me to live a good life and cherish every day how it comes. Me, being a young buck, I took that to mean for me to be the wildest dude in the world. I took his advice to mean 'do what you want to do, how you want to do it'—and I did. I lived like that, whatever I did. Whether it was drinking … everything … I took everything wrong. Like the drinking, women, living on the edge, mistreating people—I just took everything too far. By the time I realized what Uncle Charles really meant, I had spent a good part of my life living on the edge, having fun—and believe me, I had fun. I ain't one of these people who look back and say, 'Oh, man, golly, what have I done?' I had fun. The good, the bad, and the ugly—I had fun. But by the time I realized what life is all about—and thank God, thank God he saved me before I got too far that I can't recover—by the time I realized who God was and what he really meant to me, I had done lived a whole life of pursuing the wrong things. So now this is where we are right now.

"I realize now that if you are a parent or a husband, your life ain't yours. I was married, but everything had to revolve around me. I had kids, but everything had to revolve around me. Since I've changed my life and God is a part of my life, now I know I have to make sacrifices for my kids—for my wife now [Michelle]. It's kind of amazing the transformation because you just do things differently. That's basically all I can say."

"When did you find God?" I asked.

"It was once I got out of prison—you'll have to do the

research—seven or eight years ago maybe. I got out of prison and had to find a job. I went to Deion Sanders; I went to David Wells—he was a bail bondsman—and he said, 'Man I got just the guy. His name is Omar Jahwar. He's a preacher out of South Dallas.'

"I had to get a job, you see, because I was on parole in Louisiana and on probation here in Dallas, so I had to get a job or I'd be in violation. They were giving me time to get a job, and I had a big fine I had to pay back, so I went to David Wells and Deion, and they were trying to help me find a good job—not just any job. At the time, I just needed to get a job and start paying these people back their money.

"David Wells told me one night, 'Meet me at Hooters. I got this pastor I want you to meet,' and I was like, 'Whoa, meet you at Hooters? Okay.' He told me he had the perfect guy for me to meet, and he introduced me to Omar. I was like, 'I'm meeting a pastor at Hooters!' So Omar tells me he has a job for me mentoring kids in South Dallas. I said, 'What do you want in return?' He told me, 'Nothing really, but I'll think of something.' As the evening went on, Omar asked me to introduce him to Deion Sanders and ask him to come to a function to raise money for Vision Regeneration. I said, 'Well, cool, that's easy.' We spent several more hours talking in that Hooters, and it was like I had known Omar all my life. It seemed like I grew up with this dude.

"You asked me when I found God. Well, I don't know what day it was. I know most people can remember this epic day of when they recall finding God. I'm different from most people. How do you find God? God has always been there. When I decided I was going to be a part of God's plan, I was just in my truck—I think I had this little diesel deal—something small because I had just gotten out of prison. I was driving around, and I said, 'You know, God, you've always covered me through everything—multiple car wrecks, bad marriage, how I was, drug-related deals, me selling drugs, and you've always covered me. I've never really had to work a day in my life, and I've always known you. I've always known that you're about right and good—but I chose the other route.'"

Nate stopped his remembrance here and looked me right in the eyes. "I was never ignorant, you see. I always knew there was a God, but I also knew that—and here is where Dorothy and I may disagree: When I met her, I never played like I ever wanted to be a Christian. I didn't ever even say I was gonna try to be a Christian. She'll say that, through the bad times we went through, I would say, 'I'm going to try to be better,' and I would ask her to pray for me. But I was trying to be a better husband. I never said I was trying to be better with God.

"So when I decided I was going to better my life and get right with Christ, I knew I was going into it wholeheartedly, and if I saw it wasn't working, I wasn't going to stick with it. One thing about it, you're either with God 100 percent or you're going to hell.

"When I decided to change and get my life right, I was well aware of what it took because of the people around me. I knew Dorothy was a Christian; I knew my son Tré was a Christian; I knew my father, my mother, Deion Sanders, Tony Hayes, Charlie Biggers—these people were Christians. They never told me it was thunder and lightning, and all of a sudden your life just miraculously changes. I knew it wasn't like that because I knew the struggles they went through.

"So, when I became a Christian, I already knew what it was going to be like for me. I saw Dorothy, Deion, Charlie, Tony, Tré, my mother and father—I saw that they couldn't be shaken. I knew I would be like that. I told you if I believe something is right, I don't care what anybody else says or thinks. I did feel like they would probably be closer in their faith and in their walk with Christ than I could ever be — not because I started late, that isn't what determines it. Because I lived in the flesh for so long — I think if you could start earlier, you wouldn't have the habits, you see? The habits from my past ..." Nate's voice trailed off.

"What I mean is, I think with Dorothy, or Tré or Deion, they started earlier with habits of love, and the earlier you start with those habits, the easier it is if you fall off the wagon to get back on. I'm not saying they love God more than me, but they're already at the meat of the Word, and I'm just still getting past the milk and the mash. I don't have the same habits they have.

"I still have a lot of flesh to fight. The things that Dorothy went through with me — there is no way I could ever look good to someone. I would never look good to women, and I don't expect to look good. I'll deal with that. I don't need acceptance from you or anybody. All I need for you to understand is that even though I can't change what has happened, you can't stop it that now I live in peace. Who I am now, what I've been through, what Dorothy has been through, how we have come through it, how our kids have prospered — you have to let your kids know that you can change your mind. You can be different."

Nate talked for a few minutes about his parents and the differences between how he was brought up and how Dorothy was brought up. He spoke very fondly of his mom and dad and of his sons. He believed he and Dorothy shared the same basic core values all along, just that his path caused him to make very different choices.

"When I did stupid things, there were only three entities I apologized to for the wrong that I did. One was Dorothy and the boys — that's one because they are my family. Two was my mother and father. I had to apologize to them separately, you see. My mom was a schoolteacher, and I put her through a lot. My father was self-employed. He owned a store, a gas station, and several properties, and he talked and bragged about his kids. I hurt them, and I had to apologize to my parents separately. Finally, the third entity I had to apologize to was the Dallas Cowboys organization and fans. I mean, the Cowboys knew my antics — they knew — but I lived a dual life. I presented one thing and did another.

"I told some of my friends that Dorothy was going to write this book, and they told me, 'Oh, man, that's gonna make you look bad.'

"You know what? I prayed about it, and I said to myself, 'I'll deal with that when it comes.'"

We both took another sip of our coffee. I shared with Nate that the purpose of this interview was not only to lend credibility to Dorothy's story and to keep the press from doing a "he said; she said," but my main purpose in interviewing him was to reach out to those who had been abusers — men who found themselves trapped in a cycle of violence, hurting those they care about the most. I was curious about his perspective — not only on what caused him to be abusive, but even more on what caused him to stop. I wanted to know what he would say to men who abused women.

Nate dove right in. "Whether you hit a woman once or you hit her fifty thousand times, there is no place in our makeup as a man that allows for us to ever do that. It's unacceptable; that's the bottom line. Any man who knows God understands that as a man, hitting a woman is never, ever acceptable.

"Will men do that? Yes. Men will fly off the handle and do that, but I'm telling you that it is never okay. For a woman to think she has to accept that [abuse], she needs to seek help now—and much faster than that man does. For a man to beat a woman, and this is what I had to come to grips with, for a man to beat a woman, he's a coward.

"You're a coward! That's all there is to it!"

Nate took a moment to regroup. He was visibly stirred up.

"I went to God," he said, "and started seeing a change in my life, and a lot of things started to fall into place. There were things I had to do right away. I went to Dorothy right after I got out of prison and apologized to her, but I had to go back after I found God and apologize again. When I made my apologies as a Christian, only then could I even begin to understand forgiveness. Only then could I start to feel good about it. Yes, I apologized when I got out of prison, and I was grateful for the way she stuck by me and showed love, but it wasn't until I was a Christian and then made my apologies to Dorothy, to my mother and father, to the Cowboys and fans, that I began to feel good."

"Do you feel free now?" I asked.

"I do feel free, but I never want to forget and fall back into that. I have a [new] wife now. I still get mad. I still have real, real bad days and real, real bad nights, but I don't ever want to get so angry that I would put my hands on her. It takes God to keep me from that. Only God can do that.

"For athletes, I think it's worse. We're conditioned for aggression. We're conditioned to respond physically. Larry Allen [a Cowboys teammate] asked me one time, 'Nate, do you sometimes just get so wound up? So full of anxiety?' I told him, 'Yeah, I do. Let me tell you how to fix it—you gotta start praying. Don't go get a drink; don't go talk to your wife. When the anxiety attacks come, you gotta start praying. That's the only thing that's gonna fix it.'

"I tried drinkin'. I tried going away and being by myself,

but that didn't work. Nothing I tried worked. It takes God's intervention. Now I surround myself with Christians—even my doctor is a good Christian. Michelle and I have been married now for a long time. We attend North Dallas Community Bible Fellowship . . ."

Nate looked down at his watch and reminded me that he didn't want to miss the start of King's game. There is much more I want to ask him, but I know our interview has come to an end.

I'm left with the impression that this man's journey has led him to a very different place than where he was many years ago, and that he has a journey ahead of him still. I am convinced that he deeply regrets his behavior and the pain he has caused—not only to Dorothy but also to his sons, his family, and his fans. I offer a prayer for Nate as he walks out into the cold mist. I ask God to fully reveal the power of his forgiveness and acceptance to Nate. I thank God that he is faithful to complete the work he has started in Nate's life. As I watch him drive off toward Dragon Stadium, I believe that God has much, much more in store for Nate Newton.

Meet Tré and King Newton

Train up a child in the way he should go: and
when he is old, he will not depart from it.

Proverbs 22:6

My story wouldn't be complete without the perspective of my two sons, Tré and King. When I completed the initial draft of this book, I asked my friend and collaborator, Wendy Walters, to interview each of the boys one-on-one. The following is what she wrote about her conversations with Tré and King in 2011.

Tré Newton, Age Twenty-Two

I spoke with Tré over the telephone. He was very articulate but also reserved at first, unsure about what was expected of him. He knew this was important to his mom and wanted to get it right.

"What was it like for you growing up?" I asked.

"I remember lots of arguing," he began. "I would go to my room, but I still could hear what was going on. Sometimes I would pop out and see what was taking place.

"There were times I felt very helpless. I didn't know other families were different. It felt like it was wrong at the time, even though I was little, and I knew it was bad. I just didn't know any other way of life.

"When Dad started drinking, I expected something bad to happen. Like, I knew it would be bad for my mom. It hurt me, and it made me feel bad. I was used to it. It was what I expected. I knew I couldn't do anything about it.

"When it was happening, I would hide out and wait for it to be over. I knew my mom would be sad, and the next day I knew we would act like nothing ever happened.

"I knew not to say anything. I tried to avoid my dad as much as I could. I only enjoyed going with him to the Cowboys locker room because I loved football so much. At home, I never knew when he was going to go off, like he was bipolar or something.

"I have always felt real protective of my mom. I would tell her, 'Let's leave; we should go away.' I had a hard time understanding why we stayed so long. It was really bad sometimes, and I wanted her to leave. I was excited when they got a divorce."

"How has it affected you as an adult?" I asked.

"I don't want to be like that when I get older, get married, and have kids. I want to be careful to treat girls I talk to with respect. When I slip up, I think to myself, *I don't want to be anything like my dad*. I'm aware of the statistics. But I don't plan to be one of them. I have always fallen back on my faith. My mom kept us in the Word, and we always prayed together at night.

"When Mom was abused or I would be in my room praying for her that she wouldn't be hurt or that Dad wouldn't do anything, I used to pray for my dad to be a happy drunk. There were times when he was a happy drunk, and then he was actually a lot of fun to be around. When he came home drunk, I just hoped he would go to sleep. I just didn't know what to expect."

"When I spoke with your dad, he talked about how playing football had conditioned him to be aggressive," I said. "Sometimes it was difficult for him to turn that off at home. You've played a great deal of football. How did that affect you?"

"When I step onto the football field, I'm a different person. When I step off the field, that part of me shuts down."

"You saw your mom suffer for a long time. What would you tell women trapped in abusive situations?"

"My mom kept me away and protected me from the worst of it. She would send me off to my uncle T. Hayes's house or to stay with friends and try to keep me from seeing it. She would always talk to me and encourage me to talk to her. She called it 'open book time,' and it was mostly as she drove me back and forth to school. She wanted me to be able to tell her anything that was bothering me. I guess I would tell women to keep an open relationship with their kids and make sure they have permission to say anything. I knew I could tell my mom anything. I talked to my mom a lot. If nothing was bothering her, nothing bothered me. If I saw her happy, I was happy. When she was upset, I was upset. I want people to know that if they can get help, they should. There is help out there. You don't have to go through what my mom went through."

Tré changed direction a bit. "Growing up, I thought this [abuse] was normal. I know now that how I grew up isn't normal at all, but back then I didn't know anything to compare it to.

"When I was a kid, I never talked to anybody about what was going on at home—not teachers or anybody. I knew who my dad was and what he did. Family business was family business. I somehow knew I wasn't supposed to say anything to anybody else. I talked only to my mom, but nobody else. Once in a while, my dad would act out with people around, but mostly that was only around close friends, and they turned their backs and acted like it never happened. Maybe they didn't want to make him angry or rub him the wrong way. Because of who he was, they would ignore it. They wouldn't confront him."

"Have you talked to your dad about it since you grew up?" I asked.

"I have talked to my dad about the past. He'll ask me if I'm treating girls respectfully, and he really wishes that his friends would have stepped in and stopped him. I wish they would have too. Everyone was afraid because he gave them money and bought them things and took them places. I guess they thought if they confronted him, that stuff would all stop.

"I wish someone had stepped in and stopped it. Uncle T. Hayes was best friends with my dad and good friends with my mom. I think he felt that if my dad knew he knew about the abuse, it would make things worse for my mom. I think fear of what might happen kept him from stepping in."

"You know what your mom's book is about," I said. "You lived through her story and gave her a reason to survive. She is concerned sometimes about how painful your childhood was and what you remember."

"The worst memory was one terrible day. My mom drove into the driveway and told me to stay in the car. She put some music on for me to listen to. I was in the car outside, and I heard my mom and dad yelling. Stuff like, 'I can't believe you told such-and-such ...' It was really loud and really angry. I didn't stay in the car, though. I went up to where I could see through the window.

"There was my dad holding a gun, and there were two bullets on the counter. He was yelling. I remember him flipping the table over, and I thought it hit my mom in the stomach. I was really scared. Next thing I remember was seeing the window break, and I ran and got back in the car. My dad stormed out, got in his car, and left. I had always prayed for a little brother. I was scared that the baby had gotten hurt.

"You know, I used to ask my mom, 'Why can't you have another baby?' Now I understand why she was so hesitant."

Tré paused briefly.

"I'm about to graduate with a degree in corporate communications. Then I start graduate school, and I hope to get into sports management. I want to do something within sports, but I don't want to get into coaching. Any sport is okay with me, but I'm drawn to football."

"Will you continue at the University of Texas?" I asked.

"Yes, I'll do graduate school at UT. My scholarship for football doesn't run out until May 2013, so I can get a lot of my graduate school done. I was placed on medical scholarship, and I'm really grateful to be able to continue my education."

"How did you feel when you had to give up playing football?"

"That was a rough time. It still is. I've been around football my whole life. It was really hard to give it up. I knew I had to stop because I couldn't recover from concussions. You can't play football worried or scared. I started second-guessing myself. *Maybe I can avoid hits . . .* I realized then I couldn't play football if I was worried about getting hurt. When you play, you have to be all in. If you're worried about getting hit, you're going to blow it for the whole team. I was starting to feel selfish. I thought about what would happen if I ended up with permanent brain damage and how it would affect my mom.

"I'm still involved with the team, and sometimes I still think about playing. I miss it. I was really happy when I played football. I'm a student coach now. For the games, I'm in the press box and linked up with the running backs coach. I still enjoy this. I still really love football."

"You know your mother is extremely proud of you. Is there anything you would like to say to her?"

"I want her to know I love her and would do anything for her," he said without hesitation. "I think it's amazing that she was able to raise me how she did while going through all that. She came out strong. She is always looking to help others, and I hope I'll always have her same servant attitude. She doesn't even know how to be selfish. I want to take that from her."

"Is there anything you would like to say to your dad?"

"To my dad—I want to say I'm proud of him and happy. He's done a lot of wrong things in his life, but all his sins are forgiven. Stuff he did in the past—I know it still affects my mom; it still affects me, but what's done is done. At the end of the day, he's my dad, and I respect him. I'm happy he has changed and is trying to go in the right direction. I can see a big change in him. He's not the same person I grew up with at all.

"Uncle Monte and Uncle K-Mart really looked after me too. While my dad was in prison, they treated me like I was their son. I know if anything ever happened, I could go to them, and they would be there for me. While my dad was messing up, they stepped in and were role models for me. They were the ones I looked up to in order to learn how a man should treat a woman, how a man should act. I watched how my uncle K-Mart treated my auntie Lynn. My uncle Monte taught me more about the Bible and the business side of things. Uncle K-Mart taught me by example—I watched him and learned. Uncle Monte taught me by sharing his experiences. I am really grateful to them."

"Talk to me about King," I urged. "Your mom tells me he really looks up to you and admires you, that when you went away to school, it was hard for him."

"King is the person I care about most in life. I want to make sure he's alright. I would always tell King he should be thankful for how things have turned out [with the divorce]. He is mad that my dad is not around now. He has a great mom. I don't know if he really realizes how great she is. He was really little during the worst part, so I don't think he remembers much.

"King looks at other families, and it bothers him. Most of the kids in Southlake have a mom and a dad. Dad only comes around for sports. Maybe King doesn't feel like Dad cares about other parts of life—I don't know. He is longing for a father figure in his life. When I left, it bothered him. He isn't as close to Uncle Monte and Uncle K-Mart as I was. He'll be alright, though. He's got my mom, and she never gives up."

"Is there anything else you want to say? About the book release maybe?" I ask.

"Honestly, I'm not 100 percent excited about bringing up the past, but I trust my mom completely. She feels like God has told her to write the book. I trust her motive to help others—she is always about helping others—and she feels a calling on her heart to do this. I trust it will work out for the best. I'm proud of her and support her."

King Newton, Age Fourteen

I met with King and his mom on a Sunday afternoon in Dorothy's home office. I liked him from the moment I saw him. He was my kind of kid. Even though he was a somewhat reluctant interviewee, he was polite and willing to talk with me because his mom had asked him to. He was handsome, with a smile that made me melt.

King was less open than Tré had been. He sat in the chair,

slouching down, eyeing the door. "Sit up straight, King," Dorothy told him.

"What?" he answered her, smiling and chuckling.

"What can you tell me about what it was like for you growing up?" I asked. "I know you were really young when your parents divorced and your dad went to prison."

King took a moment to think. "I didn't like how other kids would bring up my dad or how he was arrested for drugs just to get at me. You know, everyone thought we were rich because my dad played for the Cowboys, and we really didn't have much. People always thought we had it made. I also didn't like that they expected me to be great at football because my dad was so good. You don't inherit sports.

"I remember going to jail to see my dad. I remember eating chicken wings from the vending machine, and that I would just go play on the see-saw while they talked.

"Some kids teased me because my dad was in jail. They would say stuff like, 'My parents told me he sold drugs and that he was a bad person.' It used to make me really mad. Some parents wouldn't let their kids play with me because of it. It didn't seem fair. *I* didn't sell the drugs!"

Dorothy chimed in. "Nate would always tell the boys stories about him and his dad. He told them all the time that his dad was such a wise man. Well, one time during a visit, King was sitting on Nate's lap, and he said to Nate, 'You always tell stories about your dad. Why didn't you ever listen to him?'" Dorothy and King both started laughing.

"That made Nate really, really mad," Dorothy said. "King knew something wasn't right; he was just too young to really understand what was going on."

"I'm kind of close to my dad now, though," King said. "I go to his house sometimes. He comes to watch me play football.

All he talks about with me, though, is football and my grades. Just football and grades. Well, my mom talks about my grades all the time too. Mostly when they're bad," he said, giving his mom an impish look.

"What about Tré being gone?" I ask.

"It's a lot different with Tré being gone. It was a lot more fun when he was around. My mom is too serious now. I text him sometimes, but we only talk when I see him. I miss having him around.

"I wish I would have been there when my dad hurt my mom," he said, changing the subject. "I would have stopped it. I would have done something. I would have told him to stop, or I would have pushed him or something. I would rather him hit me than her. I would have told the police—I don't know, something."

Dorothy's face is very soft. King is looking down at the floor, but I can see her looking at him with so much love. I don't think they have talked about this in a very long time.

"I want my mom to start dating people. I wish she would relax a little more and have more fun. I mean, she goes out with friends, but mostly she does stuff for other people, like charities and stuff. Every month, we do SASO [Scholars and Athletes Serving Others], and we also do Jack and Jill and different activities for parents, lock-ins, team building, and things like that. My mom works really hard. She always has to take care of stuff and has too much stress. I want her to have more fun. I want her to date."

"He's always telling me he wants me to start dating," Dorothy rolls her eyes.

"What do you want to be when you grow up, King?" I ask.

"I would like to go into the NFL and make some money. I would invest it in an international shipping business—you know, ship cargo and different things. I always wanted to own my own business.

"Tré was my role model," he said, shifting topics. "He's a really, really good person. I'm like the opposite of Tré. I'm talkative and happy; Tré is more secluded. He was a really good football player, though.

"I used to worry that Tré would grow up and be abusive like my dad. It would scare me when he got mad because he would yell. I watch to make sure how he talks to his girlfriend. I want him to be okay and not have anger issues.

"Me, I'm more verbal when I'm angry. I never get physical. People compare me to Tré a lot, like teachers and coaches. He was a football champion and a super student, so they expect me to be just like him, and I'm not. I'm my own person. I'm different than he is."

"King handles this really well," Dorothy interjected. "He is developing and becoming his own person, separate from Tré. Tré's expectations of King are that he should be more like him, study harder, etc. He thinks I let King get away with things, but King is very different from Tré. Every child has to be parented differently, in ways that suit their personality and gifts.

"King is the most affectionate, caring young man," she continued. "He is honest. He'll tell it all like it is without a filter," she said with a laugh. "He is very wise for his age. He came home a few years ago and said to me, 'You know what, Mom? I'm glad you work. I'm glad you share the Bible with people. If you stayed at home all the time with just me, you wouldn't reach all those people.'"

"King loves to be around people," Dorothy affirmed. "He likes crowds and is very extroverted. He wants me to remarry. He asks me about it all the time. I think he just wants a man around on a more regular basis. He notices things going on in other people's lives, and when he comes home, he'll tell me who we need to pray for. I just really want the best for him."

King shoots her another look, admiration mixed with something like, *You're really embarrassing me.*

"Am I done?" he asks.

"Alright, alright. You can go," Dorothy says.

King is out the door, quick as lightning.

"Young man," Dorothy says with that "Oh, no you didn't" tone of voice, "you come back here. You shake Mrs. Wendy's hand. Tell her thank you. Where are your manners?"

"Sorry, Ma," he calls out, coming back to shake my hand. "Thanks!"—and he's gone.

Why Won't She Leave?

The cold facts are that one out of four women in America will experience some type of domestic violence in their lifetime. Obviously, the safest choice is always to leave a dangerous or threatening situation, but many victims do not feel they can make this choice. Here are some reasons a woman might choose to remain in an abusive situation.

Nurturer by nature. Many women struggle to place their own well-being above the love they have for their partner. For women who are nurturers by nature, leaving can seem like a selfish choice.

Economics. Most families require two incomes to survive. For many women, the man is still the chief breadwinner. Some women work only part-time or not at all. Concerns over how to provide for housing, transportation, clothing, shelter, and education are among the top reasons for staying with an abuser.

Custody. Losing custody of children is one of the greatest reasons cited for staying. When money is an issue, a mother faces a genuine fear that she will not be able to keep custody. Leaving the children to live with an abuser, unable to be there as a buffer or to protect them, is a legitimate concern. This causes many victims to put up with whatever they have to in order to remain close to their kids.

Shame. Shame and the fear of isolation are powerful restraints. Victims are often convinced they did something to cause the abuse. They also believe they can do something that will make it stop. Physical abuse often leads to sexual abuse, even within the confines of marriage. This is a very difficult thing for a woman to talk about.

Denial. Because abuse is cyclical, there are often seasons of calm or even "good times." In the calm times, it can seem as if things have changed, maybe for good this time. Many women believe each abusive episode will be the last. They convince themselves that the worst is over and abuse will never happen again. The longer the time lapse between episodes, the harder it is to leave.

No hope. For a woman trapped in abuse, the situation seems hopeless. She feels trapped, and she's convinced that she has no choice but to suffer. Although this is not the case, in her mind she has no choice because no alternatives make sense. The emotional damage she experiences is severe. It cripples her self-esteem and renders her powerless to make decisions, particularly as they affect her own health, safety, and well-being.

How Do I Help Her?

Build her up. When a woman shares her situation with you, even when she is unwilling to reveal all the details, it is important to acknowledge her feelings and stress that the abuse is not her fault. She does not deserve to be punished by abuse. Let her know that what she is going through is terrible, but she doesn't have to go through it alone—you are with her and for her. Give her the confidence of knowing that you will stick with her, no matter what she decides to do. Let her know that you are a safe place where she can come to talk and, if necessary, to have action steps put into place to intervene.

Remind her that she has choices, and give her strong encouragement. Affirm her for sharing her situation with you, and note how it demonstrates that she is doing something right. Resist the temptation to say things like, "What you need to do is …." or "If anyone ever hit me, I would …." Such statements only damage her self-esteem more. It is easy to say what you would do or what she should do, but you are not the one suffering the abuse. If you were, you might see things less clearly.

Pray. Pray *for* her, and pray *with* her. Pray for her safety and that of her children. Pray that God would intervene in the life of her abuser. Just knowing that someone is praying can bring enormous encouragement to her soul.

Help her create a safety plan. Helping her create a safety plan is one of the most valuable and empowering things you can do. The website for the National Domestic Violence Hotline (www.thehotline.org) provides practical guidance for a variety of situations, including safety planning with children, pets, during pregnancy, and while living with an abuser. You can also call anonymously, and they answer the phones 24/7. The number is 1-800-799-SAFE (7233). Their staff is available to assist victims (and anyone calling on their behalf) with crisis intervention, safety planning, and referrals to shelters and agencies in all fifty states. They offer valuable information for victims and victim support, as well as someone to talk to who can provide help.

Help her create a financial plan. An important part of creating an action plan is assessing potential financial resources. A loss of financial support is one of the chief reasons women remain with their abusers. Help her assess what she has available, and put a plan in place to set money aside, develop job skills or seek employment, access financial assistance through government or charitable organizations, and perhaps even speak with family members who might support her while she gets on her feet. Helping her develop a workable financial plan to support herself without her abuser's income will empower her and allow her to make better choices.

Be trustworthy and remain supportive. It may take some time before an abuse victim is ready to take action. It can be difficult to remain patient and understanding when you know someone you care about is living with abuse. But trying to compel her to act before she's ready may place her at increased risk of abuse. You must be sensitive and aware. However, if you believe her life is in immediate danger, contact the authorities. Then be prepared to stand by her until she is safe from harm. Victims of abuse have difficulty trusting other people. Betrayal is real to them, and they have been repeatedly hurt by someone they love. It is important that you be trustworthy. If she confided in you, it was a big step for her. Take your cues from her, and make sure she knows she can always trust you and rely on you.

Encourage her to learn self-defense. Learning self-defense techniques is a valuable skill set for everyone, but it can make the difference between life and death for victims of abuse. Depending on the situation, it may not be possible for a woman to take a self-defense class, but resources are available that can help. For example, the National Domestic Violence Hotline website (www.thehotline.org) encourages women to make themselves a small target by curling into a ball and to avoid wearing scarves or long jewelry that might be used for choking or strangling. Identifying available resources (online and in the community) may help her to defend herself and limit the damage from a physical attack.

Encourage her to grow in self-awareness. It is very important for a victim of abuse to become self-aware. She can combat the emotional damage inflicted by her abuser by deflecting the ugly words and reminding herself of her value and worth. This is easier said than done, but the greater her self-awareness, the less power the abuser has over her. You can help by reminding her of her value and affirming her in her strengths. If she is a Christian, encourage her to take refuge in God's Word. Filling her mind with the truth of what God says about who she is will help deflect the damage of what her abuser says about her. This is a powerful practice that should not be underestimated.

I Am Being Abused. What Should I Do?

Reach out to others. First, know that you are not alone. You are the victim. One out of every four of your women friends has also experienced some type of domestic violence. Being abused is not your fault. Don't isolate yourself by shutting people out. Isolation is dangerous. You need to reach out to someone and let them know you need help. You have someone who can and will help you—a friend, a family member, a church, or an abuse shelter.

If you are uncomfortable speaking with a friend or family member, call the National Domestic Violence Hotline at 1-800-799-SAFE (7233). You can call them anonymously. There are people available 24/7 to answer questions, direct you to local assistance, or just to talk. For additional information, access their website at www.thehotline.org. You'll find practical information to help you protect yourself now and to create a plan if and when you decide to leave.

Reach up to God. Calling on the Lord is not a platitude or a last-ditch effort. He does protect, defend, comfort, deliver, and heal. Spending time with him, meditating on his Word, and worshiping him can bring hope and great inner strength when you need it. It will also fill your mind and heart with truth. Believing the lies and negative things an abuser has said during a shouting match serves only to lower your self-esteem and give your abuser power over you. Shouting back is a natural response, but it only escalates the abuse.

Instead, focus on what God says about you by trying to see yourself through his eyes. Dare to believe his promises and the grace-filled truth that he has a destiny for your life that no one should ever be given the power to deny. You are beautiful. You are unique and special and one of a kind. You are precious in God's sight. He esteems you highly and has numbered the very hairs on your head. He is grieved when you suffer, and he captures your tears in remembrance. Reach up to him. Call on him. He is always there.

Why Do Abusers Abuse?

It is easy to sympathize with a victim and easier still to vilify an abuser. What makes someone abuse another human being? Why do some people turn to violence and cruelty, particularly with people they love?

Research clearly demonstrates that abuse patterns repeat for generations. If children were abused or witnessed a loved one being abused, they are much more likely to grow up and be abusive. Watching cruelty go unpunished or internalizing values that violence is normal and acceptable contributes to this generational curse. Likewise, victims of childhood abuse are more likely to seek out unhealthy or dysfunctional relationships in which they again become victims.

People who deal with emotional discomfort through addictive behaviors such as alcohol, drug abuse, unrestrained shopping, and gambling are more likely to become abusive. Abuse itself becomes an addiction. It is a coping mechanism.

Abusers tend to deny their responsibility, even when they

come back and apologize. They'll say, "That wasn't really me," or "I just lost control"—or some similar excuse—rather than try to repair the damage or change their behavior. No matter how excessive the abusive behavior is, they seem to find a way to excuse it. They blame a "trigger" event, not their lack of self-control, for the violent outburst. Unless and until abusers can accept personal responsibility for their actions—for choosing to harm another person—little can be done to help them.

Abuse victims sometimes say that on the day after an abusive episode, abusers often seem to have little or no memory of what occurred. They act as if nothing ever happened. Stranger still, abusers often demonstrate outrage at the abusive behavior of others, without recognizing similarities in their own abusive tendencies and behavior.

Abuse tends to go in cycles. It begins with a buildup of tension, followed by a violent outburst, the denial of responsibility, an apology driven by guilt, and then a period of calm. Then the cycle repeats itself and can continue for years.

Abusers demonstrate behavior that is egocentric and self-absorbed. They see the world only as it impacts them and have little awareness of how they impact their world. They excuse their violent behavior as a legitimate response to the injustice or unfair treatment they have received. Their demands are self-centered, and their need to control their victims is obsessive. Having to cover up their bad behavior leads to lies and deception, a lifestyle pattern that is difficult to reverse.

The good news is that abusers can change. But they cannot do it alone. If you are an abuser, or if you recognize abusive tendencies in yourself, one of the best first steps you can take is to seek the support of a qualified counselor. You also need an accountability structure. Find a close friend—not your spouse—with whom you will be honest and who you know will be honest with you. Ask them to meet with you regularly and to hold you accountable for your actions. Give them permission to intervene if you violate your partner through violence again.

Ultimately, your avenue for deliverance and restoration is the same as it is for every other human being, which is a surrendered relationship with God. God's love and forgiveness are available for you. His forgiveness isn't partial; it is complete, total. It covers all your sins, not just select sins. You can be forgiven. God can deliver you, heal you, redeem you, change you, and give you the opportunity to lead a whole, functional life.

Nate Newton found God. It was not until after the divorce and his prison sentence that he came to the reality that he was never going to be "good enough" through his own efforts. He needed God to step in and cleanse him. But he chose to change, to let God change him—and you can too.

Maybe you consider yourself a Christian and wonder why you remain abusive. Have you admitted your sin? Acknowledged your guilt? Have you repented and asked for God's forgiveness? Have you accepted his sacrifice, believing it is sufficient for you? Do you understand that the same grace that covers lying and stealing and adultery and murder also covers cruelty and violence and abuse? Sin is sin in the eyes of God. Total forgiveness and amazing grace provide an opportunity to live free again. Jesus paid the price for you. You have but to receive his sacrifice.